MICHAEL
CRICHTON

Other titles in the Greenhaven Press Literary
Companion to Contemporary Authors series:

Tom Clancy
John Grisham
Stephen King
J.K. Rowling

The Greenhaven Press
LITERARY COMPANION
to Contemporary Authors

MICHAEL CRICHTON

Robert Hayhurst, *Book Editor*

Daniel Leone, *President*
Bonnie Szumski, *Publisher*
Scott Barbour, *Managing Editor*

**GREENHAVEN
PRESS ®**

San Diego • Detroit • New York • San Francisco • Cleveland
New Haven, Conn. • Waterville, Maine • London • Munich

LIBRARY OF CONGRESS CATALOGING-IN-PUBLICATION DATA

Readings on Michael Crichton / Robert Hayhurst, book editor.
    p. cm. — (The Greenhaven Press literary companion to contemporary authors)
Includes bibliographical references and index.
ISBN 0-7377-1663-0 (pbk. : alk. paper) — ISBN 0-7377-1662-2 (lib. : alk. paper)
    1. Crichton, Michael, 1942– . Criticism and interpretation. 2. Science fiction, American—History and criticism. I. Title: Michael Crichton. II. Hayhurst, Robert, 1974– . III. Series.
PS3553.R48Z76 2004
813'.54—dc21   2003044858

Printed in the United States of America

CONTENTS

Foreword   8

Introduction   11

Michael Crichton: A Biography   14

Chapter 1: Profiling Michael Crichton

1. The Early Career of a Prolific Writer
   by Israel Shenker   33
   As a medical student, Crichton wrote novels under a
   pseudonym. He first found fame with *The Andromeda
   Strain*, his first novel written under his own name.

2. Moving Across Mediums
   by Malcolm Jones, Ray Sawhill, and Corie Brown   39
   Hollywood producers and booksellers are often challenged by Crichton's versatility and refusal to keep doing the same type of book over and over again.

3. A Career in Three Acts *by David Kippen*   42
   Michael Crichton's career mirrors the construction of a
   hit Hollywood movie.

Chapter 2: Crichton's Books

1. *The Terminal Man*'s Fascinating Technology and
   Solid Plotting Are Marred by Poor Character
   Development *by Theodore Sturgeon*   56
   While *The Terminal Man* is aided by fascinating de-
   tails, its poor character development weakens what
   could have been a great book.

2. *Sphere* Delivers Terror Through Precision Crafting
   by James M. Kahn   59
   Crichton uses such care and precision when relaying
   the details of *Sphere*'s undersea setting that when leaps

of the imagination are made, the reader suspends all disbelief.

3. What Makes *Jurassic Park* So Suspenseful
   by Elizabeth A. Trembley   62
   Crichton builds and maintains suspense in *Jurassic Park* by separating his characters into groups, then shifting focus from group to group.

4. Shadow World *by George F. Will*   68
   Rising Sun presents a distorted picture of Japanese influence in America. The result is a boring novel.

5. *Rising Sun:* Japan-Bashing for the Masses
   by Mike Tharp   72
   Rising Sun relies on "revisionist" experts to achieve a sense of scholarship. Consequently, its conclusions are based on outdated and misleading information and express hatred toward the Japanese.

6. *Disclosure's* Caricatured Characters and a Clunky Plot Derail a Potentially Effective Satire *by Julie Connelly*   75
   In the hands of a stronger writer, *Disclosure* would have made a great satire. But the novel is derailed by one-dimensional characters and a plodding plot.

7. *Timeline* Is the Laudable Product of a Great Craftsman—Not an Artist *by David Klinghoffer*   79
   Three elements are necessary for great craft novels: mystery, twists, and a ticking clock. Crichton is a master at incorporating these elements into his books.

8. *Timeline:* Seductive Ideas Undermined by a Formulaic Narrative *by John Dugdale*   83
   Although it presents interesting ideas, *Timeline* is peopled with shallow characters and contains many battle and action sequences, turning the novel into a quasi-video game.

9. *Prey* Is Vintage Crichton with a Few Firsts
   by Ned Vizzini   86
   Crichton does a good job of portraying American family life in the first half of *Prey*, then switches to his real forte: creating a compelling technological crisis with a

roller-coaster of action scenes and plot twists. He also attempts a few firsts, like writing from the first-person point of view.

Chapter 3: Crichton's Films

1. Crichton on Directing *by Gary Arnold*   91
   The skills Crichton learned in medical school served him well while directing films. Like doctors, directors must adapt to new tools and processes and anticipate problems.

2. Movies Cannot Be Scientifically Accurate
   by Michael Crichton   97
   When featuring scientists and science, Hollywood films cannot be wholly accurate because their primary concern must be to tell a good story.

3. *Jurassic Park:* Imagining Dinosaurs in the Modern World *by Don Lessem*   107
   The real-life model for *Jurassic Park*'s Doctor Grant scrutinizes the realism of the film and the book and discusses the possibilities of making a real Jurassic Park.

For Further Research   118

Index   123

FOREWORD

Contemporary authors who earn millions of dollars writing best-sellers often face criticism that their work cannot be taken seriously as literature. For example, throughout most of his career, horror writer Stephen King has been dismissed by literary critics as a "hack" who writes grisly tales that appeal to the popular taste of the masses. Similarly, the extremely popular Harry Potter books by J.K. Rowling have been criticized as a clever marketing phenomenon that lack the imagination and depth of classic works of literature. Whether these accusations are accurate, however, remains debatable. As romance novelist Jayne Ann Krentz has pointed out:

> Popular fiction has been around forever but rarely has it been viewed as important in and of itself. Rarely have we acknowledged that it has a crucial place in culture. . . . The truth is, popular fiction—mysteries, science fiction, sword and sorcery, fantasy, glitz, romance, historical saga, horror, techno-thrillers, legal thrillers, forensic medical thrillers, serial killer thrillers, westerns, etc.—popular fiction is its own thing. It stands on its own. It draws its power from the ancient heroic traditions of storytelling—not modern angst. It is important, even if it is entertaining.

Although its importance often goes unrecognized, popular fiction has the power to reach millions of readers and to thus influence culture and society. The medium has the potential to shape culture because of the large and far-flung audience that is drawn to read these works. As a result of their large readership, contemporary authors have a unique venue in which to reflect and explore the social and political issues that they find important. Far from being mere escapist fiction, their works often address topics that challenge readers to consider their perspectives on current and universal themes. For example, Michael Crichton's novel *Jurassic Park*, while an entertaining if disturbing story about what could happen if dinosaurs roamed the planet today, also explores the potential negative consequences of scientific advances and the ethical issues of DNA experimentation. Similarly, in his 1994 novel *Disclosure*, Crichton tells the story of a man who suffers predatory sexual harassment by his female supervisor. By reversing the expected genders of the victim and aggressor, Crichton added fuel to the debate over sexual politics in the workplace.

Some works of fiction are compelling and popular because they address specific concerns that are prevalent in a culture at a given time. For example, John Grisham has written numerous novels about the theme of corruption in America's oldest legal and business institutions. In books such as *The Firm* and *The Pelican Brief*, courageous though sometimes naive individuals must confront established, authoritarian systems at great personal danger in order to bring the truth to light. Written at a time when government and corporate scandals dominated the headlines, his novels reflect a faith in the power of the individual to achieve justice.

In an era when 98 percent of American households have a television and annual video sales outnumber book sales, it is impossible to ignore the fact that popular fiction also inspires people to read. The Harry Potter stories have been enormously popular with both adults and children, setting records on the *New York Times* best-seller lists. Stephen King's books, which have never gone out of print, frequently occupy four to five shelves in bookstores and libraries. Although literary critics may find fault with some works of popular fiction, record numbers of people are finding value in reading these contemporary authors whose stories hold meaning for them and which shape popular culture.

Greenhaven Press's Literary Companion to Contemporary Authors series is designed to provide an introduction to the works of modern authors. Each volume profiles a different author. A biographical essay sets the stage by tracing the author's life and career. Next, each anthology in the series contains a varied selection of essays that express diverse views on the author under discussion. A concise introduction that presents the contributing writers' main themes and insights accompanies each selection. Essays, profiles, and reviews offer in-depth biographical information, analysis of the author's predominant themes, and literary analysis of the author's trademark books. In addition, primary sources such as interviews and the author's own essays and writings are included wherever possible. A comprehensive index and an annotated table of contents help readers quickly locate material of interest. In order to facilitate further research, each title includes a bibliography of the author's works and books about the author's writing and life. These features make Greenhaven Press's Literary Companion to Contemporary Authors series ideal for readers interested in literary analysis on the world's modern authors and works.

INTRODUCTION

Michael Crichton is no stranger to the best-seller list. In fact, he is more like a longtime resident. Almost every one of his novels has been a best-seller, starting with the first book he published under his own name: *The Andromeda Strain.* Crichton is no stranger to Hollywood either. Almost every one of his novels has been made into a successful film, and he is the creator of the popular *ER* television series. Having rejected a career in medicine, Crichton went on to top three of the main barometers of popular culture: the best-seller list, the box office, and the Nielsen ratings.

Of course, Crichton is best known for his monster hit *Jurassic Park.* Steven Spielberg's film version became one of the highest-grossing films of all time and brought Crichton added fame. The story features dinosaurs who are brought to life through cloning and wreak havoc on an island theme park. Crichton has written other books that warn of the dangers of science run amok, such as *The Terminal Man* and *Prey.* But although compelling, this subject matter does not account for Crichton's success or popularity. His best-sellers cover such diverse topics as medieval Europe, Japanese economics, talking gorillas, sexual harassment, a Victorian robbery caper, and aircraft manufacturing. Readers seem to buy his books no matter what the subject. So although Crichton has been called the father of the modern techno-thriller, it is not technology that accounts for his success.

How then does Crichton create such compelling fiction? How does he manage to create best-sellers from such disparate subjects? There are two special, crucial skills that

Crichton wields perhaps better than any other modern writer. First, he possesses an uncanny ability to synthesize complicated ideas into terms that lay readers can understand. Second, Crichton writes with an innate understanding of cinematic storytelling.

Crichton tackles any subject that interests him. The more complicated, the more varied, the better. Whereas many authors write only in a single genre, such as science fiction or horror, Crichton defies categorization. Readers do not know what kind of story they will encounter when a new Michael Crichton book comes out. So when Crichton embarks on a new adventure into uncharted territory, he knows that many of his readers will be unfamiliar with the areas they are about to explore. He carefully explains the technicalities and nuances of the world of the novel, usually by speaking through characters who have expertise in the areas that need clarification. Readers are soon made to feel comfortable in the novel's surroundings. Crichton writes with such authority, readers suspend their disbelief and follow the story through even the most complicated and unlikely scenario—such as dinosaurs come back to life. In a novel like *Timeline*, for example, Crichton deftly handles the double challenge of educating readers about both the nuances of quantum mechanics and medieval life in fourteenth-century France.

Crichton's second crucial skill is his mastery of cinematic storytelling. His innate understanding of movie-style story structure is apparent in all of his works, no matter the subject. Crichton frequently weaves multiple plotlines together, often using an episodic style that checkerboards cliff-hangers and mini-climaxes, quickly moving the story forward and urgently building toward a powerful ending. Such structures are the hallmark of many great Hollywood films. In *Jurassic Park*, for example, Crichton is constantly shifting focus among his groups of characters, thereby enabling readers to experience more action and excitement than would be realistic for one group alone. This tactic is mirrored in the film version. Many literary critics applaud Crichton's cinematic sensibilities. But some critics contend that Crichton's books read more like screenplays than novels, and that Crichton writes with future films in mind. In his defense, Crichton insists that his style of writing is inherently cinematic, similar to that of Robert Louis Stevenson, author of *Treasure Island.* Crichton says he simply describes the pictures that he sees in his head.

One philosophy in Hollywood holds that a good movie is like a horrendous train wreck that begins with well-built locomotives barreling toward each other from a great distance. Crichton's skills are like well-built, fast-moving locomotives. When they collide, compelling fiction emerges from the flames.

MICHAEL CRICHTON: A BIOGRAPHY

*"He has maybe the richest imagination of anybody I know.
And he grounds his fantasy in such contemporary technical reality that he can make the reader swallow just about
anything."* —Steven Spielberg

*"Someone once compared me to a bat. 'Put a bat among
birds,' he said, 'and they call it a mammal. Put it among
mammals and they call it a bird.' In more intellectual circles, I'm seen as a 'popular entertainer' unworthy of consideration. In popular entertainment circles, I'm considered too intellectual. I don't seem to fit in anywhere."*
—Michael Crichton

For a man who doesn't fit in anywhere, Michael Crichton has
found success just about everywhere. He has excelled
academically, studying anthropology at Harvard, then gradu-
ating from Harvard Medical School. He has directed several
films, including such successes as *Westworld, Coma*, and *The
Great Train Robbery.* He created the perennial television hit
ER. But he is best known for his blockbuster novels, which
have made his name a commodity in the entertainment industry. Books like *Jurassic Park, The Terminal Man, The Andromeda Strain, Sphere, Rising Sun*, and *Disclosure* have all
been wildly successful. Each has been made into a successful
movie, creating a hunger in Hollywood for anything Crichton. Whenever he writes a new book, studios pay millions of
dollars for the rights to turn Crichton's creation into a film.
Not surprisingly, he is one of the richest entertainers in the
world. Michael Crichton is a big man who casts a long

shadow, both figuratively and literally. But this creative giant almost followed a completely different course—that of medicine. Discovering and heeding his true calling would prove an arduous path.

Crichton was born on October 23, 1942, in Chicago—half a mile from the hospital where television's *ER* is set. He grew up in Roslyn, Long Island, New York, the eldest of four children—two boys and two girls. His mother, Zula (Miller) Crichton, was a homemaker. His father, John Henderson Crichton, was a corporate president and an executive editor at *Advertising Age* magazine.

Crichton's parents encouraged their children to pursue a wide variety of interests. Theater, museums, and movies all played large roles in family life. Crichton says, "It was an idea in my family that it was good to have an interest in many diverse things—that you didn't have to have a scheme whereby it all fit together."

FAST START

Crichton's father fostered a love of writing in his children—three of the four children have published books—and he encouraged Crichton to submit a travel article to the *New York Times* when he was fourteen. To Crichton's surprise, it was accepted and published—and Crichton had made his first professional sale. He was paid sixty dollars, which supplied him with pocket money for a year. The piece was inspired by a family vacation to the huge meteorite crater near Winslow, Arizona. Entitled "Where the Meteor Scarred Arizona's Desert," the article goes into great depth about meteorites and illustrates Crichton's lifelong penchant for science. Even this early writing gives a good indication of Crichton's future writing style: clear, concise, fact filled, with a dramatic atmosphere.

Inspired by the success of his first attempt at professional writing, Crichton wrote and submitted many more pieces to a variety of publications over the next three years. However, none of them was published.

A STRAINED RELATIONSHIP

Despite the influence his father would have on his future as a writer, Crichton's relationship with his father was strained. Crichton felt not only encouraged to succeed but also driven. Even as a young boy, his achievements were scrutinized. For example, as a third-grader, Crichton wrote a nine-page script for a puppet show. His father criticized it as the most clichéd thing he had ever read. His father was not only harsh at times, but he could also be violent. As Crichton writes in his autobiographical book, *Travels*, "My father and I had not had an easy time together. We had never been the classic boy and his dad. And it hadn't gotten better as we got older. . . . As far as I was concerned, he was a first-rate son of a bitch."

At times, Crichton hated his father, whose words and actions created a great deal of tension in the family. Crichton was also saddened that his father hid emotions like love and respect. The tension and pain of his relationship with his father affected Crichton for decades. Crichton never reached an understanding with his father while his father was alive. Only after his father's death, during an out-of-body spiritual experience, did Crichton discover the understanding and acceptance he had longed to share with his father throughout his life.

GROWING UP TALL

Another source of awkwardness growing up was Crichton's height. He was six feet seven inches tall by the time he was thirteen. Other children sometimes teased him because of his height. He would eventually grow to six feet nine inches. Crichton's height has always given him a remarkable presence, especially on movie sets and in interviews; in fact, Crichton's height is usually mentioned when features about him are published. Crichton once met Wilt Chamberlain, the famous basketball player. The experience of meeting the seven feet two inches Chamberlain helped Crichton put his own height into perspective. Crichton eventually came to embrace his height. "I had to admit," he says, "that part of me is proud of what makes me different."

CHILDHOOD PASSIONS

One of Crichton's childhood passions was technology. Crichton's brother recalls that Michael spent a lot of time in the backyard gazing up at the sky through a telescope he had constructed. In high school, Crichton was also a member of the school's rocket club, which was especially popular during the 1950s after the Soviet Union launched *Sputnik*, the world's first satellite.

Another of Crichton's loves was film. When his parents took him to see Alfred Hitchcock's *To Catch a Thief,* Crichton was hooked. Seeing the film proved to be one of the greatest moments of his childhood. He soon developed a love for the magical world of movies. He learned about Hitchcock and was amazed that one could make a living creating movies. His fascination with Hitchcock would later lead Crichton to direct several movies himself. In fact, one of his films, *Coma*, would go on to be praised as a Hitchcockian film. Although Crichton would initially pursue a career in medicine as a young man, his interest in film never left him.

At Roslyn High School in New York, Crichton became a basketball star. Many of the records he set there still stand today. He also studied Latin and was a student journalist. "Roslyn was another world," Crichton says. "Looking back, it's remarkable what wasn't going on. There was no terror. No fear of children being abused. No fear of random murder. No drug use we knew about. I walked to school. I rode my bike for miles and miles, to the movie on Main Street and piano lessons and the like. Kids had freedom. It wasn't such a dangerous world."

GOING TO COLLEGE

After high school, in 1960, Crichton enrolled at Harvard. He intended to become a writer like his favorite authors,

Edgar Allan Poe, Arthur Conan Doyle, and Robert Louis Stevenson. However, he discovered that the English department was "not the place for an aspiring writer; it was the place for an aspiring English professor." He was also dismayed to be receiving C- grades for work he thought to be well above average. He decided to test the Harvard grading system. Crichton put his own name on an essay written by George Orwell, who wrote such classics as *Animal Farm* and *1984*. The essay received a B-. "Now Orwell was a wonderful writer," Crichton says, "and if a B-minus was all he could get, I thought I'd better drop English as my major."

Crichton promptly changed his major to anthropology, took premed courses, and graduated summa cum laude. After graduation, Crichton lectured in anthropology for a year at Cambridge University in England. He also received a Henry Russell Shaw fellowship, which allowed him to travel around Europe and North Africa. When he returned to America, he enrolled at Harvard Medical School. From 1964 to 1969 Crichton labored through the academic challenges of becoming a medical doctor.

DISILLUSIONMENT WITH MEDICINE

Medical school marked a turning point in Crichton's life. Up until this point, his studies were a pursuit of knowledge and learning, which Crichton found stimulating. But in medical school, he discovered an entirely different attitude. The environment was not only competitive but also hostile. There was no real emphasis on instilling a sense of compassion in the future doctors. Crichton was bothered by an environment in which, for example, his fellow students would engage in such activities as playing a game of laboratory football with human livers. He also had to fight the urge to faint whenever he drew blood.

His first rotation in neurology revealed the startlingly cruel underbelly of a profession he had entered in order to care for others. In *Travels*, Crichton discusses witnessing the chief resident sadistically prodding patients with pins to test for consciousness. In the maternity ward, some nurses often refused to give painkillers to unwed mothers. He felt he had entered some level of hell from Dante's *Inferno*. The women were "all twisting and writhing in rubber-sheeted beds," Crichton says, "all shrieking at the top of their lungs in the most hideous agony."

These experiences shaped his perception about the scientific and medical professions. He would later explore the failings and arrogance of these professions in such books as *Jurassic Park, The Terminal Man, The Andromeda Strain, Congo,* and *Sphere*. He soon came to the conclusion that "how a doctor behaved was at least as important as what he knew."

THE PSEUDONYM NOVELS

As an undergraduate, Crichton's family had supported him financially. But Crichton paid his way through medical school by turning to his first career choice—writing. He used three pseudonyms during these years: John Lange, Michael Douglas, and Jeffrey Hudson. The latter is a pun on Crichton's height. In reality, Jeffrey Hudson was an eighteen-inch dwarf courtier of King Charles II.

While in medical school, Crichton was producing about one book a year, and soon two. He wrote steadily on weekends and often finished his books during his two-week Christmas breaks, getting paid just in time to pay for the next year of medical school.

Crichton's first novel, written in 1966 when he was twenty-three, was a pornographic thriller called *Odds On*—a caper in which thieves rob a resort hotel using their knowledge of statistical probability. It features many of the characteristics of future Crichton novels, including a race against a ticking clock and a richly detailed single setting. *Odds On* was followed up by *Scratch One*, then *Easy Go* (later republished as *The Last Tomb*), in which a band excavates a long-lost Egyptian burial chamber.

Next was *A Case of Need*—the first Jeffrey Hudson book. This mystery thriller made a case for legalized abortion. It tells the story of a young Chinese American obstetrician charged with performing an illegal abortion on the daughter of a prominent Boston surgeon. It is also Crichton's first book to address a timely and controversial topic—a characteristic that would surface again in such best-sellers as *Jurassic Park, Disclosure, Rising Sun,* and *Airframe. A Case of Need* won the 1968 Edgar Award from the Mystery Writers of America. It was also Crichton's first book to be made into a movie. Blake Edwards directed, James Coburn starred, and the film was renamed *The Carey Treatment.*

In 1969, a busy year, Crichton took the Hippocratic oath and became a licensed physician. He also published *The Venom Business,* a book about smugglers using false-bottomed cobra cages to hide contraband. That year he also published the Hitchcockian *Zero Cool.* But Crichton's most important professional achievement to date was the 1969 release of the wildly successful *The Andromeda Strain.* This was his first best-seller, and it was published under his own name. The novel describes an alien bacteria that lands on Earth, killing people as it spreads. It was considered salient at the time, as the world pondered the threat of potential alien microbes brought back by astronauts who were just beginning to visit the Moon. The book was the first of several to appear at just the right time, echoing some issue of society that happened to be a hot topic. The same luck would help ensure the popularity of books like *Jurassic Park, The Terminal Man, Rising Sun, Disclosure,* and *Airframe.* The success of *The Andromeda Strain* indicated to Crichton that perhaps he could make a living writing novels.

A few pseudonym books were published even after *The Andromeda Strain,* including *Grave Descent, Drug of Choice,* and *Binary,* a strongly crafted novel about a nerve gas scare in San Diego that some critics quietly argue is Crichton's best book. In 1971 Crichton cowrote a comedic drug satire novel with his brother, Douglas. *Dealing: Or, the Berkeley-to-Boston Forty-Brick Lost-Bag Blues* was published under a single name, Michael Douglas.

Most of the books Crichton wrote under pseudonyms are out of print and are hard to find. Two exceptions are *A Case of Need*, which was republished under Crichton's own name in 1994, and *Binary*, which was republished in 1994 as part of a collection with *Rising Sun* and *The Andromeda Strain*.

QUITTING MEDICINE

Throughout medical school, Crichton had been leading a kind of double life. He had been concerned with the rigorous academic demands of learning to become a doctor. But he had also found some success as a professional writer—something he had wanted to be since childhood.

An imbalance was growing between the two worlds of medicine and writing. Not only was Crichton experiencing increasing disillusionment with the medical establishment, but his success as a writer was growing, seemingly tempting him to follow this new path that was, at the same time, a return to the path he had longed to follow since he was a boy. The publication of *The Andromeda Strain* had suddenly thrust Crichton into the limelight. Seemingly overnight he was a twenty-seven-year-old best-selling author. And he had more money than he had ever had before. He did not need to write thrillers anymore in order to pay for medical school. With the sale of the film rights to *The Andromeda Strain*, he had enough money to afford just about any luxury he desired. But he tried to take it all in stride. He continued his studies, and he continued to write.

Crichton was also finding it challenging to balance medical school with his newfound fame as a writer. Some professors supported his writing, but others thought he was wasting his time. Still others thought he was wasting their time, suspecting he was not serious about becoming a medical doctor. In either case, many believed he should not try to be both a medical student and a writer but should instead choose one profession.

He also found himself listening to his patients' stories with an ear toward gathering material for his new books. Realizing he had a conflict of interests, Crichton decided he would earn his medical degree but would not become a practicing physician. When Crichton told his colleagues that he planned to leave medicine to pursue his writing career, he was met with skepticism and discouragement. People thought his dreams were unrealistic. As he wrote in *Travels*, "To quit medicine to become a writer struck most people like quitting the Supreme Court to become a bail bondsman." However, when his peers discovered that Crichton was the author of the best-selling *Andromeda Strain* and had sold the rights to the book to Hollywood for $250,000, they encouraged him.

During this time Crichton began experiencing a strange numbness in his right arm that lasted for several weeks. Soon his legs were also tingling. Harvard's best doctors examined Crichton and agreed that he had multiple sclerosis, a progressive, degenerative disease that often leaves its victims immobile. Crichton knew that if he had only a few productive years remaining, he wanted to spend them doing what he loved—writing. This incident reaffirmed Crichton's conviction that his decision to leave medicine was correct.

Since that initial attack, Crichton has experienced no further episodes of numbness or tingling. He is unsure whether he experienced a single attack of multiple sclerosis or an intense anxiety reaction to his decision to leave medicine.

CRICHTON BREAKS INTO FILM

Crichton began his journey into film even before quitting medicine. As *The Andromeda Strain* was being filmed at Universal Studios in Hollywood in 1970, Crichton was fulfilling a one-year research fellowship at the Salk Institute in La Jolla, California, near San Diego. Crichton was even given a tour at Universal by a young up-and-coming director working there—Steven Spielberg. Crichton took advantage of every opportunity to drive up to Universal and watch the production of *The Andromeda Strain*, a big-budget movie at the time at 6 million dollars. Robert Wise, the film's director, allowed Crichton to haunt the set, learning what he could about the moviemaking process. Crichton also attended Hollywood parties and met actors. He began to file away mental notes about actors' behavior patterns and the complaints they most often expressed about directors.

In 1972 Crichton also observed the filming of two more of his novels: *Dealing* and *The Carey Treatment* (from *A Case of Need*). Crichton decided that he too could direct a film. He negotiated his directorial debut into the contract of his next novel. He was given permission in 1972 to direct *Pursuit*, a television movie based on his novel *Binary*. After *Pursuit*, Crichton wrote the screenplay for the Jeannot Szwarc film *Extreme Close-Up*, a softcore pornography film about high-tech surveillance. In 1973 he wrote and directed his first theatrical feature, the well-received and successful *Westworld*, a film about a futuristic theme park where robots go berserk. The film was the first ever to feature computer-generated special effects. *Westworld* was also released in a paperback version in 1974.

The success of *Westworld* enabled Crichton to direct a well-received adaptation of Robin Cook's medical thriller *Coma*. Next Crichton directed *The Great Train Robbery*, based on his own book by the same name. It became another successful film and starred Sean Connery, who became a close friend. The success of *Westworld*, *Coma*, and *The Great Train Robbery* led many critics to believe that Crichton was an up-and-coming force as a director. Unfortunately, the films that Crichton next directed proved disappointing. *Looker, Runaway*, and *Physical Evidence* all had less-than-stellar performances at the box office.

Even as Crichton was making a move into movies, fulfilling a second lifelong dream, he continued to write at a furious pace. He wrote a well-received nonfiction book about American medical care called *Five Patients: The Hospital Explained* (1969). His next thriller was *The Terminal Man* (1972). With the success of *The Andromeda Strain* and *The Terminal Man*, Crichton's reputation was set as an author who understands science and technology and their dangers.

Crichton followed *The Terminal Man* with *The Great Train Robbery* (1975), a novel set in Victorian England about a carefully planned theft aboard a steam locomotive. Even this book demonstrated Crichton's knack for writing the right book at the right time. Few were interested in the Victorian era as Crichton was writing the book, but the period experienced a coincidental revival as *The Great Train Robbery* was published.

In 1976 Michael Crichton wrote the catalog text for a retrospective exhibit of the works of renowned artist Jasper Johns that was featured at the Whitney Museum. *Jasper Johns* proved to be a book with "legs"—it remained in print for many years, and Crichton updated it to include information on Johns's new paintings.

A Bump in the Road

When Crichton's next five books were published, they were not particularly successful at the time. Crichton's popularity diminished. To make matters worse, he developed a bad case of writer's block during the late 1970s and early 1980s. Writing became very difficult for him. No matter what he tried, nothing seemed to help. The period lasted about five years, then went away.

Crichton's first notably unsuccessful book was *Eaters of the Dead*, published in 1976. The story combines elements of the epic poem *Beowulf* and the historic accounts of Ibn Fadlan's experiences with the Vikings. Crichton wrote the book as a kind of bet that he could make *Beowulf* into an interesting narrative story. He found it a very technically challenging book to construct. He was conducting a great deal of research, but he was also inventing scholarly data to round out the story. At times, even Crichton became confused about which references were real and which he had made up, a situation he found extremely frustrating.

From 1976 to 1980 Crichton did not publish any new books. Instead, he traveled all around the world, gathering many experiences that would later work their way into Crichton's autobiographical *Travels*. In exploring Buddhism, he realized that by growing up and living in only one culture, his interactions with others were somewhat stilted. His experiences spurred him to travel even more widely in the coming years and to explore new realms, both physical and spiritual. He realized that his travels enabled him to access deeper aspects of himself. As he wrote in *Travels*, he developed an "almost obsessive desire for experiences that would increase [his] self-awareness."

In 1980, still battling his case of writers block, Crichton published *Congo*. He had always been fascinated with H. Rider Haggard's adventure story *King Solomon's Mines*. Crichton wrote *Congo* as a kind of twentieth-century version of a Victorian jungle adventure story while simultaneously exploring animal-human communication. It would be seven years until he would publish his next novel. Crichton did write an unusual little book in 1983 called *Electronic Life*. It was written as a layperson's guide to computers and how to think about them.

Crichton finally returned to fiction with *Sphere*, published in 1987. The story features an ensemble of scientists trying to unravel the mystery of an unidentified craft discovered at the bottom of the ocean. The book was not very successful at the time it was published. However, after Crichton published *Jurassic Park*, *Sphere* enjoyed a strong revival. It was later made into a successful film directed by Barry Levinson and starring Dustin Hoffman, Samuel L. Jackson, and Sharon Stone.

In 1989 Crichton published *Travels*, his first autobiographical book. It details his experiences and adventures in far-flung locations around the globe, such as diving with sharks and climbing Mount Kilimanjaro in Africa. As Crichton was writing the book, he began to feel more comfortable. He soon delved into increasingly personal material, including his rocky relationship with his father and the wide array of spiritual experiences that changed his outlook on the world and the nature of reality.

With these five books, Michael Crichton had somewhat disappeared from radar screens. Neither his movies nor his books were generating much attention.

SUCCESS REDISCOVERED

When *Jurassic Park* was published in 1990, it was instantly successful. After a long absence, Crichton had finally returned to the best-seller lists. The book was timely, too. It was published as new strides were being made in the scientific fields of microbiology, such as the Human Genome Project, a massive effort to unravel the blueprint of the human makeup that began in 1990. But with the 1993 release of Steven Spielberg's film version of *Jurassic Park*, one of the biggest blockbusters of all time, Crichton enjoyed a huge resurgence in popularity and a renewed interest in all of his books. Naturally, *Jurassic Park* became a runaway best-seller again and shot back atop the best-seller lists. *Jurassic Park* has spawned a follow-up novel, three movies, video games, toys, and movie merchandise.

The seeds of *Jurassic Park* go back to 1983, when Crichton was working on a screenplay about a pterodactyl brought to life through the cloning of fossilized DNA. The screenplay did not work, but Crichton eventually rewrote it as a novel about dinosaurs run amok in a theme park. The novel was originally written from a boy's point of view. When he showed it to the half-dozen close friends to whom he routinely shows his early drafts, they complained that they wanted a story written more for adults. Crichton rewrote the story, focusing more on the adult characters. Crichton's confidants loved it— and so have millions of readers around the world.

Crichton followed up *Jurassic Park* with two more best-sellers: *Rising Sun* (1992) and *Disclosure* (1995). Both books were hits, both were made into hit movies, and both were controversial. *Rising Sun* depicts an investigation of a call-girl murder set against a backdrop of questionable Japanese multinational practices. *Disclosure* explores a high-tech corporate environment where a man sues a woman for sexual harassment.

In 1994 *ER*, Crichton's television show about life in an urban hospital, debuted on NBC. It became an instant hit. Crichton is one of the show's executive producers. He was heavily involved with the show for the first couple of years, but since then he has become more hands-off and has enjoyed the show more as an avid viewer. It took almost twenty years for *ER* to get made. Crichton developed the idea as a documentary-style movie after writing and directing *Westworld*. He updated the script every five or ten years, but it was always rejected by the studios and networks. Finally NBC made and aired the pilot episode, and the series was born.

In 1995 Crichton revisited his dinosaurs. The title for his *Jurassic Park* sequel, *The Lost World*, is taken from Arthur Conan Doyle, one of Crichton's favorite writers. Steven Spielberg directed the hit movie based on the book. Soon after, Crichton and his wife, Anne-Marie Martin, cowrote the screenplay for the hit movie *Twister*, which was released in 1996.

For some years Crichton had wanted to write a novel that featured the complexities of aircraft manufacturing. *Airframe* is a novel about the airliner industry, with a subplot about the voracity of an often-unethical television media. Fortunately for the book's sales, it was published in 1997 during a time when a number of airline accidents and incidents propelled aviation safety into the forefront of public discussion. Again, Crichton had written the right book at the right time.

Another longtime desire of Crichton's was to write a time-travel adventure story. The only other novels that he had set in the past were *The Great Train Robbery* and *Eaters of the Dead*. But his next novel, *Timeline*, featured modern-day graduate students from the present propelled into the past, forced to confront a world completely alien to them. In this way, Crichton could explore the past through the eyes of contemporary characters, so readers could more readily identify with the story. Sent to the Dordogne region of southwestern France during the 1300s, Crichton's protagonists must rescue their professor, who has been trapped in this war-torn medieval alternate universe.

Prey was published in 2002. Unlike *Jurassic Park*, which features very large organisms (dinosaurs), *Prey* focuses on the very small. It explores the world of nanotechnology, a new scientific field that is still highly theoretical. It involves the manufacture and programming of microscopic robots that may one day be capable of, for example, traveling through the human bloodstream and conducting "repairs" on vital organs or clearing arterial plaque. In the story, a cloud of these minute machines escapes from a Nevada laboratory and begins behaving like a larger collective organism, a predator. Like *The Terminal Man* and *Jurassic Park*, it echoes basic questions about the potential influence of technology on humans.

SPIRITUAL MATTERS

One less well-known aspect of Michael Crichton is his interest in spirituality and metaphysics. He does not discuss these topics often because many people's reactions are less than open-minded. When Crichton was directing *The Great Train Robbery* in England, he began visiting psychics and spiritualists to explore an old interest: the connection between the body and the power of the mind. For several weeks, he experienced psychic readings. For every reading, he wanted to determine if the spiritualist had genuine powers or was simply picking up on subtle information he might be conveying accidentally. So each time, he purposefully withheld clues—both verbal and nonverbal—that might reveal certain information to the spiritualist. The accurate readings that the spiritualists gave him convinced Crichton that there was a genuine phenomenon at work, though he could not be sure exactly what it was or how it worked. Intrigued, he explored other metaphysical phenomena, which he details in his autobiographical *Travels*. He witnessed the healing power of laying on of hands. He saw auras. He "heard" a cactus speak. He visited a past life as a gladiator in ancient Rome. He bent spoons and forks into wildly contorted shapes using only the slightest touch. He compared the feeling of the metal to slightly warm, pliable plastic.

One experience that was particularly intense and poignant came when Crichton experimented with out-of-body travel. He came to an astral plane where he encountered the spirit of his father, who had died years earlier. At first Crichton was very anxious because of the strained relationship he had had with his father in life. But his perception changed immediately when the spirit embraced him. "In that instant of embrace," Crichton says in *Travels*, "I saw and felt everything in my relationship with my father . . . all the love that was there between us, all the confusion and misunderstanding that had overpowered it. . . . My relationship with my father had been resolved in a flash."

FAMILY AND HOME LIFE

Michael Crichton has been married and divorced four times. He married his high school sweetheart, Joan Radam, in 1965, when he entered medical school. They divorced in 1970 after moving to southern California. In 1978 Crichton married Kathy St. Johns. They were divorced in 1980. He later married Suzanne Childs, a public relations representative for the Los Angeles District Attorney's Office. Next he married Canadian actress and screenwriter Anne-Marie Martin. During their fourteen-year marriage, Martin once said of Crichton's intense work habits, "It's like living with a body and Michael is somewhere else." Crichton and Martin divorced in 2003. Martin blamed Crichton's frenetic work schedule for the demise of the marriage. Crichton and Martin share custody of their daughter, Taylor Ann.

Crichton once discussed marriage in an interview with *Playboy:*

> I have learned that marriage is hard, but it's good for me. I've also learned that both people need to have a commitment. The moment one person doesn't want to be there, it gets difficult. You should want to spend a lot of your leisure time together, sharing the same interests. You may not see the person all week, but when Saturday rolls around, if she wants to go shopping and you want to go hiking, you have a problem.

Crichton lives in a modest bungalow in Santa Monica, California. He once lived in a canyon-top house that had reflecting pools, glass pavilions, and manicured lawns. His current home is much more livable, he says. Very few changes were made to the house when Crichton moved in. He describes the home as a place where one can put one's feet up on the furniture and put drinks down without worrying about condensation rings or scratches. Crichton does not care much for socializing, finding it mundane, believing time spent with his family is more important. He reads about three hundred books a year and enjoys movies, tennis, diving, and fast cars. He also has an extensive collection of modern and primitive art that features works by such artists as Rene Magritte and Roy Lichtenstein. His art collection has been sent on tours to various museums.

MORE BOOKS TO COME

For over thirty years Michael Crichton has churned out novels that have gripped the imagination of well over 100 million readers. His ideas have touched millions more through movies like *Jurassic Park* and his television show *ER.* His reputation as the father of the techno-thriller was set with the publication of *The Andromeda Strain*. But he has since gone on to even greater achievements, becoming a permanent resident of the best-seller list, directing several successful films, writing screenplays, and creating video games and a hit television program. The future looks bright for the man with an imagination so gifted he has become one of the world's most popular writers. Luckily for his readers, Crichton shows no signs of running out of gripping, blockbuster ideas.

CHAPTER 1

Profiling Michael Crichton

READINGS ON
MICHAEL CRICHTON

The Early Career of a Prolific Writer

Israel Shenker

In this *New York Times* feature, writer Israel Shenker profiles Michael Crichton in June 1969, at the beginning of what would become Crichton's juggernaut career as a bestselling author, director, producer, and screenwriter. Crichton discusses the challenges of balancing medical school, writing, and newfound wealth and fame. He also details the tactics he used while writing *The Andromeda Strain*, much of which was influenced by Len Deighton's novel *The Ipcress File*.

If there is a bigger literary property these days than Michael Crichton (rhymes with frighten), where will the money come from? Within the past six months, young Crichton (he is 26, stands 6 feet 9 inches, and is in his fourth year at Harvard Medical School), has:

Finished *The Andromeda Strain*, which is Book-of-the-Month Club co-selection for June and has been sold to Universal for $250,000;

Written an original screen play called *Morton's Run*, which has also been sold to Universal;

Fulfilled two-thirds of a contract for three original paperbacks;

Written a prospectus for a TV series, and a two-hour script for a pilot show;

Continued work on a nonfiction study of the Massachusetts General Hospital;

Done magazine articles;

Started four novels and two screen plays;
Steeled himself to hear the worst about his seventh
book—*The Venom Business*—to be published July 15.

When the cash register clicked more slowly, during his
sophomore year at Harvard College, he tried basketball as
well. Crichton likes to win and Harvard usually loses, so he
quit while they were behind.

WRITING AT HARVARD

Crichton writes summers, during Christmas vacations—and
sometimes when he should be at class or clinic. "It's a bit like
epileptic seizures," he said. "This spring I freed myself from
classes and I wrote like a fiend."

Because of his height he is exempt from the draft. Since
doctors, however, are drafted whatever their altitude, he will
not become an intern. "Anyway," he says, "as you go on in
medicine the conflict of interest grows between the demands
of writing and commitment to your patients."

"At medical school a number of people find it intriguing
that I write," said Crichton, "and have always been well dis-
posed. The dean always reads my books. A few of the teachers feel I'm wasting my time, and that in some way I've
wasted theirs. When I asked for a couple of days off to go to
California about a movie sale, that raised an eyebrow."

CHANGES COME WITH FAME

"These months have been explosive, but I consider everything that happened as external to me. All I did was write a
book, and the publishing bandwagon super-phenomenon
has nothing to do with me. It's occasionally disturbing to
meet people who can't see beyond this person who's at medical school, who's made a lot of bread writing novels, and
who's famous.

"I'm not going to buy a yacht or a gold lamé suit or di-
vorce my wife. She was working to put me through medical
school, and every time the money was about to run out it

was time to write another book. That gets dreary, especially because I wasn't writing good books.

"So it's of great concern to me to get some distance from this hand-to-mouth thing, although I've found that Galbraith was right: there's an enormous difference between not having enough and having enough, and no important differences between having enough and having more than enough.

"I'm interested in exposure. If there's something you want to say, no matter how wild, the best way is television. More people will see one lousy television show in a night than will see a good movie in a year. More people will see a lousy movie in a week than read a good book in a year."

EARLY START

That commercial message might—or might not—go down well with Crichton's father, who is president of the American Association of Advertising Agencies. At dinner the children—all keen on writing—would discuss English usage. "I remember writing scripts for puppet shows in the third grade," said Crichton, "and long short stories in the sixth grade. When I was 14 I sold an article to the travel section of *The Times* and got $60. It kept me in money for a year."

WRITING IN EUROPE

He worked just hard enough at Harvard College to be graduated summa cum laude, and was awarded a $3,000 travel fellowship. Crichton left for England, and found himself teaching a semester of anthropology at Cambridge University—and measuring the Elgin Marbles for anthropological purposes.

"I picked up *The Ipcress File*," he recalled, "and was terrifically impressed with it. A lot of *Andromeda* is traceable to *Ipcress*, in terms of trying to create an imaginary world using recognizable techniques and real people.

"Between [Len] Deighton and [Ian] Fleming the spy business was booming. It appeared to me that almost any idiot could write a spy-story, and I discovered that almost any idiot can—although I never finished the first one."

His fellowship forbade him to stay more than two months in a place, so he moved on to the rest of Europe. By the time he reached the Riviera he was married (a girl from back home in Roslyn, New York) and torn between the lures of the Cannes Film Festival and the Monaco Grand Prix. "I decided any idiot should be able to write a potboiler set in Cannes and Monaco," he said, "and it took me 11 days."

USING PSEUDONYMS

"The book was so good," he added. But N.A.L. published it as *Scratch One*, giving the author's name as John Lange. An Andrew Lang used to write fairy tales; Crichton had added an "e" to Lang and substituted his own first name (which he otherwise never used) for Andrew.

Crichton decided on a pseudonym so that future patients would not believe he was interested in them for his plots instead of their pains. He became addicted to pseudonyms when he decided his output appeared too great for a single author. His fourth book—*A Case of Need*—for example, boasted a new pseudonym: Jeffery Hudson. The name belonged earlier to a dwarf in the court of Charles I who was served to his monarch in a pie and later captured by Barbary pirates.

The Mystery Writers of America awarded the book an Edgar—as the best mystery published in the United States in 1968, and film rights were purchased by Herb Alpert, whose Tijuana Brass had turned to gold.

"My feeling about the Lange books is that my competition is in-flight movies," said Crichton. "One can read the books in an hour and a half, and be more satisfactorily amused than watching Doris Day. I write them fast and the reader reads them fast, and I get things off my back."

DEVELOPING *THE ANDROMEDA STRAIN*

For *The Andromeda Strain* he was willing to slow down. "The idea was in my mind for at least three years," he said, "and I was trying to write it for a year and a half, collecting newspaper clippings and research articles, and writing draft after draft. Every draft was awful. What I was up against was the very considerable absurdity of the idea of a plague from outer space. When I finally learned that a complicated quarantine procedure really existed for the U.S. moon program, it was a considerable psychological boost, and then I knew I could do the book.

"People have compared *Andromeda* to *Fail-Safe*, but it's the exact reverse. *Fail-Safe* describes an event with great immediacy, as though it could happen at any moment. You are there and it's now. I found you could make something more believable if you pretended not that it might happen or was happening, but that it had happened. You are not there, and it's over.

"The secret of the success is that the appropriate tone was found and rigorously adhered to. And then there was an enormous amount of luck."

LOOKING TO THE FUTURE

Crichton plans to push his luck, and has even considered a third pseudonym—a woman's name—to see how amusing it would be to write from a woman's viewpoint. He may call herself Marie Antoinette (court of Louis XIV), whose goose was cooked by a cake and who was later captured by Bastille pirates.

Whether as Lange or Hudson or Antoinette or even the essential Crichton, he has become less indulgent about his facility for generating 10,000 words each 15-hour working day as he heats up potboilers that are never watched very long. He would like to write seriously about: euthanasia (he favors it), abortion on demand (ditto), marijuana (he wants it legalized), and the battered baby problem (he gropes for words to express his shock). He is already serious enough about reading (300 books a year) and seeing other people's movies (60 a year).

For a change of climate and scenery, he and his wife are moving to California after his graduation from medical school. One immediate project is a joint novel with his 19-year-old brother, Douglas, a junior at Harvard. "It's about youth and drugs," said the older Crichton. "I wrote it completely from beginning to end. Now he's rewriting it from beginning to end, and then I'll rewrite it completely. Eventually we'll have a book.

"Since Douglas is concerned about anonymity, we'll probably call the author *Time* magazine."

Moving Across Mediums

Malcolm Jones, Ray Sawhill, and Corie Brown

The authors of this *Newsweek* profile explain that Michael Crichton moves easily from novels to screenplays to television shows. However, this versatility displeases Hollywood movie moguls, who would love him to continually clone *Jurassic Park*–type stories—in other words, big, bankable blockbusters. In fact, even booksellers' strategies must be flexible when it comes to Crichton. Each new book might explore a completely new topic, so Crichton cannot be pigeonholed like other best-selling writers who continually churn out similar stories featuring recurring franchise characters.

Standing beside Michael Crichton amid the armor collection of New York's Metropolitan Museum of Art, you get a vivid sense of his creative power. He has the ability to take the relics of a museum case, objects that have been boring children on rainy Sundays for generations, and turn them into *Timeline*, his fascinating new novel about time travel back to 14th-century France. Crichton is a master of an odd hybrid: entertaining novels that educate. *Timeline* is a page turner and a very lucid look at life in the late Middle Ages. He teaches you how to think like a knight during a joust by putting you in the saddle. You're balancing a lance in one hand, a shield in the other, while you struggle not to fall off a galloping horse and struggle even harder not to throw up in your helmet.

PRISONER OF SUCCESS?

But this exhibit also inspires another question: does Crichton, at 57 the most financially successful novelist of the day, ever feel like a prisoner of his own success, trussed up like one of these knights in shiny but not very flexible armor? Typically, he mulls over the question for several seconds before he answers. "There is an internal and an external pressure to keep doing the same thing," he says slowly. "People liked it. You got rewarded and praised for it. So do it again! The same, only different. So it becomes something you have to fight."

That's a battle Crichton never stops fighting. While he moves easily from fiction (*Jurassic Park*) to original screenplays (*Twister*) to television ("ER"), media moguls keep nagging aloud, how do you get a handle on a best-selling writer like this who won't settle down and create a franchise like Tom Clancy's Jack Ryan? Even booksellers, who love Crichton, point out that you don't sell him the way you sell Grisham or Clancy, where you know going in what you're going to get. Crichton's audience, they say, changes with every book. As a result, say executives at Knopf, the selling strategy changes, too. "Will it be like *Disclosure*, or more like *Jurassic Park*?" says marketing director Paul Kozlowski. "Sci-fi or mystery?"

Crichton's versatility makes his stock in Hollywood a little shakier, partly because he produces the occasional bomb, like last summer's *The 13th Warrior*. But Hollywood's real problem with Crichton is that he doesn't just keep doing *Jurassic Park* over and over. "His name sells movies," says one studio chief, "but it has to be a blockbuster idea. He's not a guarantee." That problem arose again last month when it briefly appeared that Crichton's new manager, Michael Ovitz, couldn't sell *Timeline* to the movies. Because Crichton has a spotty box-office record? Because a lot of people want to see Ovitz fail? Choose both. And while Ovitz sold the book to Paramount, the chattering continued. The potentially lucrative deal Ovitz won for Crichton on *Timeline* reflects that opinion: $1 upfront, but as much as 15 percent of the gross. In other words: when we make money, you make money.

Crichton says the *Timeline* deal worked out "exactly as I wanted," and there is no doubt that even in his business dealings, he is a creative contrarian. He gets away with that because he is powerful, and because he's known as a stand-up guy. According to Disney studio head Joe Roth, when Crichton saw that Disney was never going to get his novel *Airframe* into production, he recently made the unprecedented move of buying back the rights for $1 million less than the $10 million Disney paid for it three years ago.

Timeline is a novel about arrogance—modern arrogance (we're smarter than people were 500 years ago) and 14th-century arrogance (you build a suit of armor to deflect arrows, and then they shoot the horse out from under you). In Crichton's view, arrogance leads to stasis and antiquation. His way around the problem is to keep moving intellectually, no matter what the cost. "I think if you don't fail a certain percent of the time, it means you're playing it too safe. You're obligated to miss sometimes." And somewhere, hearing that, a producer—probably someone Crichton helped make rich—is throwing up in his helmet.

A Career in Three Acts

David Kippen

Writer David Kippen breaks down Michael Crichton's career into three acts, echoing the formula for Hollywood screenplays and films. Crichton's early books are explored in great depth, as well as the professional slump that he endured in the 1980s before reaching his greatest fame. Crichton candidly answers a variety of questions in an interview format.

Boy finds gelt, boy loses gelt, boy get gelt back.

Fittingly for the boy who's spawned four Hollywood blockbusters in three years, Michael Crichton's career follows the three-act Hollywood structure perfectly. First came the ascent: From a pseudonymous writer of efficient potboilers, Crichton became the 1970's preeminent purveyor of sophisticated entertainments of which neither reader nor filmgoer needed to feel ashamed. Then the lean years intervened, roughly concurrent with the Eighties, when a couple of iffy books and three ham-fisted movie thrillers had him widely written off as written out. But the current decade finds him back atop both the best-seller lists and, less directly, the box office charts, with newfound primacy in the Nielsen ratings besides. Hardly anybody even mispronounces his name, which rhymes with "frighten," any more.

Of these three acts, the first is by far the most intriguing, because least known. Born in Chicago almost 55 years ago, Crichton grew up tall and gifted in Long Island. His father edited *Advertising Age* magazine for a time; his mother was, as *Variety* has it, nonpro. Crichton got on the scoreboard early with a piece for the travel section of the *New York Times*. It paid $60, not bad for a 14-year-old. He studied at Harvard with the class of 1964 and must have liked something about it, because he soon re-upped for med school.

But by 1966 he was off track. Between classes he sold a pornographic thriller called *Odds On* to New American Library, which brought it out as a paperback original. A caper story about thieves who knock over a resort hotel using a thorough knowledge of statistical probability, *Odds On* already bears many hallmarks of the mature Crichton's methodology: a tight clock, sure command of a single setting, and a roughly handled femme fatale. It also marks the earliest instance of a minor but impressive skill: Michael Crichton consistently finds (or invents) some of the most apt epigraphs in contemporary fiction, not just to open his books, but sprinkled generously between chapters as well.

CARVING CADAVERS AND CHURNING OUT THRILLERS

While Crichton was carving up cadavers, his fictive alter ego John Lange was churning out thrillers at the rate of first one a year, and soon two. The forgettable *Scratch One* preceded *Easy Go*, later republished as *The Last Tomb*, in which another typical Crichton rogue's gallery teams up to excavate a long-lost Egyptian burial chamber richer than Tutankhamen's. A sense of humor absent from too much of his later work lightens up the skullduggery, as when one character, told the dog statue he's just been playing catch with actually represents the formidable Egyptian death god Anubis, pats its head and whispers, "Nice doggie."

Crichton changed styles as well as pseudonyms for his first thriller of ideas, *A Case of Need*. The former high-school basketball standout puckishly borrowed the name of Jeffery Hudson, a dwarf courtier to Charles II, to tell a realistic Boston-set mystery that simultaneously made a case for legalizing abortion. It won him the Edgar Award from the Mystery Writers of America and his first brush with Hollywood, where Blake Edwards cast James Coburn in it and filmed it as *The Carey Treatment.* (The studio later took it away from Edwards, and the result wasn't pretty.)

The Venom Business found Crichton back under the John Lange shingle, rushing through a story of international criminals who smuggle contraband in false-bottomed cobra cages, thus dissuading any overzealous customs agents. That same busy year, 1969, he took the Hippocratic oath as a licensed physician and published a second Lange novel, the cryptically titled and really quite enjoyable *Zero Cool,* an outlandish Hitchcockian toss-off about a feckless radiologist who comes between a nefarious, aftershave bottle–collecting count and a priceless emerald. The climax, not always a strong point in Crichton's work, takes place in Spain's Alhambra and still ranks among his best.

1969 is also the year Crichton said goodbye to life as a private citizen, as it saw Knopf's publication, under his own name, of the fantastically successful novel *The Andromeda Strain.* Around the time the world was trying to deny its disappointment at finding out the moon was just an abnormally large moon rock, along came a book that suggested something was out there after all, and that bringing it back might not be the smartest idea we've ever had. No less an authority than Tom Clancy called it the first techo-thriller, and Robert Ludlum has been ringing variations on its title for his entire career.

John Lange books continued to trickle out even after his breakthrough: *Grave Descend,* a virtual rewrite of *Zero Cool* with a nefarious collector of Samuel Johnson editions in pursuit of shark-menaced undersea treasure; *Drug of Choice,* about a kind of narcotically-induced Club Med, where wealthy tourists tan shoulder-to-shoulder under poultry lamps and return home raving about the greatest vacation of their lives; and, finally, *Binary,* about a nerve gas scare in San Diego circa 1972. Only a heretic would suggest that the last-named novel, combining an unfailingly surprising plot, an authoritatively presented warning against chemical weaponry and the two most fully characterized adversaries in the whole Crichton canon, remains his best book.

Crichton adapted *Binary* into a tense, corking 90-minute made-for-TV film called *Pursuit*, which became his directorial debut. He also wrote the screenplay for the Jeannot Szwarc film *Extreme Close-Up*, an interesting failure that uses the format of a softcore porn film to make its ulterior points about high-tech surveillance, in much the same way he now uses thriller conventions to advance his ideas about genetics, Pacific Rim trade or air safety. *Pursuit* won Crichton the right to helm his first feature, the ingenious *Westworld* (whose screenplay came out in paperback soon thereafter), and from there the record becomes increasingly public.

He wrote *Five Patients: The Hospital Explained*, a well-reviewed work of nonfiction about American medical care, and with his brother Douglas wrote what remains his funniest book, the drug satire *Dealing: Or the Berkeley-to-Boston Forty-Brick Lost-Bag Blues*. For his follow-up thriller to *Andromeda*, Crichton turned from H.G. Wells' turf to Mary Shelley's, penning *The Terminal Man* and cementing his reputation as a novelist whose supple understanding of science and technology does little to alleviate his mistrust of it.

On the film front, Crichton followed the success of *Westworld* with well-received adaptations of Robin Cook's *Coma* and his own *The Great Train Robbery*, the book his dedicated readers tend to remember most fondly. And then, as Crichton himself might put it in one of his signature one-word paragraphs. . . .

Disfavor.

SECOND-ACT REVERSAL

In a sobering second-act reversal, *Eaters of the Dead, Congo, Electronic Life* and *Sphere* went from the best-seller list to the remainder table. *Looker, Runaway* and *Physical Evidence* followed January openings with early spring video releases. As I wrote in *Boxoffice* magazine when *Physical Evidence* came out, "Michael Crichton would have made a lousy surgeon. He leaves gaping holes in his work, he's shaky where precision is needed, and, with *Physical Evidence* now dead on the table, the blood of another thriller dries brown under his fingernails. . . . Did Crichton decide against a promising career as a knife just to become a hack instead?"

Its hard to say just where Crichton went wrong in the Eighties. Perhaps his parallel successes in fiction and filmmaking left him confused about which medium best suited each project, or the collapse of MGM/UA, the combine that financed *Westworld, Coma* and *The Great Train Robbery*, knocked him off his cinematic stride.

ACT THREE

Regardless, the curtain did not begin to lift on Crichton's third-act redemption until his 1988 collection of autobiographical musings, *Travels.* Though not a barn-burning commercial success, perhaps the mere exercise of writing something that couldn't possibly become a movie somehow recharged his batteries. Whatever the reason, *Travels* contains some of Crichton's best, funniest prose, including a terrific, fight-starting essay about how women are the cruder sex and men the more romantic. "Each sex assumes the opposite sex is just the way they are," Crichton declares. "So women think men are explicit, and men think women are romantic. Eventually that becomes a stereotype that nobody questions. But it's not accurate at all."

After that came the best-selling *Jurassic Park, Rising Sun* and *Disclosure*, all of which became movies, the majority of which became hit movies, and the first of which redefined "hit" completely. Children and family figure in all of them to a greater degree than in any of his previous work, and the reason isn't difficult to discern. Crichton got married for the fourth time a few years back, and became a father for the first. His wife, Anne-Marie Martin (who played Hooker at Bar in *Runaway*—you remember), collaborated with him on the screenplay for *Twister*, which was making money even faster than *Jurassic Park* for a while there.

What Crichton will do next is no easier to predict than it ever was. "ER," the series he and Steven Spielberg created, continues to thrive. Spielberg just finished directing the *Jurassic Park* sequel, *The Lost World*, whose title Crichton pinched from his beloved Conan Doyle. In 1996 Crichton burned up the best-seller lists all over again with a thriller about flight safety called *Airframe*. He hasn't even ruled out directing his own work again.

DR. ROSS

At this point in his career, there seems only one thing Crichton can't do, and that's the one thing he's never been able to do: Give a character an interesting name. It's getting embarrasing. Space and mercy forbid an exhaustive catalog of the flat, boring, unimaginative names Crichton has given his characters over the years. Let it suffice to note that "ER," *Congo*, *The Terminal Man* and *Zero Cool* all feature a protagonist named Dr. Ross. Can't a writer this prodigiously talented think up a new name? Failing that, can't a man who owns a piece of "ER" afford a telephone directory?

This has become so maddening that finally there was nothing for it but to drop by his Santa Monica office and ask him about it.

FIRST: For an inventive guy, you have some of the most boring character names around. I've counted four Dr. Ross so far. Is that by design?

MICHAEL CRICHTON: I use the same name twice as a way to emphasize artifice. It's like an artist using the same image in multiple prints. It's a way to say, "It's not real." Having used a name before, I would use it again as a way to say that the previous use—I don't know how to say it—that the name doesn't mean anything. It's not a real name, see?

Here it is again, in another context, in another gender.

But people are making connections where I'm trying to break them, so I stopped it. The high point of this was *Congo*, where I changed all the factual information. My idea was to do a written equivalent of a Rousseau painting, where these jungle plants were all artificial and they don't have any correspondence to nature. I was trying to make a text that would be like Rousseau. That was my idea. But in fact, all that happened was, people said "these facts are all wrong." So I kind of had to give that idea up. What I was trying to do by making these changes was not getting across.

ARTISTIC INFLUENCE

F: *Binary* is dedicated "To Jasper Johns, whose preoccupations provided solutions." Do you think the effect of art on your work has been underestimated?

MC: I made a lot of references to Duchamp in *Sphere*. I was facing a problem, in that there's supposed to be this alien spaceship, and I wanted it to have the quality that it seemed to be organized in some odd way. If I did the organization of the spaceship, then it would reflect my mind, and that was the way the whole rest of the book was, because I was writing it. So I was trying to impose a structure that wasn't mine. Therefore I used a lot of references to Duchamp's work, and to his painting called "The Bride Stripped Bare by Her Bachelors," even. I think it does have a kind of weird, alienating effect on the readers.

F: *The Andromeda Strain* can be read as a pastiche of *War of the Worlds*, and *The Terminal Man* of *Frankenstein*. Are your models as explicit as they used to be?

MC: I don't imagine that what I'm doing is pastiche-like. I actually have the goal of taking a very familiar form and re-working it. In almost everything I can think of, I'm trying to revive a form which is so familiar that it's dead and just say, "It's not dead." That means that you're always playing on the border of cliche. I have to be.

F: Did art influence your filmmaking career?

MC: At the time I was directing, I felt I was reacting against an emerging period of extremely aggressive directorial styles. The clearest example then—he's more muted now—is Scorsese. All of those very active camera movements drew attention to the fact that there was a person telling you the story in a very specific way, and you were being asked to recognize how it was being told to you. I didn't want to do that. I wanted to do a much more self-effacing directorial style. That was my goal. I think now there's a sort of exhaustion with aggressive directing. Everyone is so camera-zippy. In fact, this whole trend of stunning camera work has been very much influenced by commercials, and directors coming out of commercials. I think it's kind of played out. If you didn't know, could you differentiate Michael Bay (*The Rock*) from Adrian Lyne (*Fatal Attraction*) from Alan Parker (*Evita*)? Could you really? I don't think so. These guys are doing a similar kind of very heightened visual stuff, which is very exciting, but it's not individual, like Hitchcock or Wellman. It's not.

COLLECTING

F: Do you collect books or just write them?

MC: I've just started collecting books, actually, with these beautiful old editions of Jules Verne. My wife started getting them for me as presents, and they're so lovely. It made me interested in collecting books.

F: How are you going about it?

MC: She's actually doing it. I'm just enjoying them.

F: Surely you don't paw through first editions of Jules Verne with your bare hands? Or do you?

MC: Absolutely. It's a book. I think objects are to be used, you know. I collect old watches, and I wear them, but I won't collect a watch that I can't wear.

F: In some of your early books, you're even writing about collectors. The villain of *Grave Descend* even collects Samual Johnson first editions. How do you feel about those books?

I know you didn't put your name on them. . . .

MC: I feel that something is done for a certain purpose. The idea for those books, those early books, was to defray the cost of my medical education. They were original paperbacks. They were not, in my mind, intended to last. I wasn't writing them for the purpose of having them be around decades later, I was writing them as a very much disposable thing, almost like a long magazine article. They weren't getting the time I would give something now, they weren't getting the attention. The whole idea was something completely different from what I do now.

F: Are you ashamed of them?

MC: No, but I've opposed their reissue. I think it would confuse people now to see them, because they're not what I do now. I felt the same way about a later book, which was intended to be a catalog for a Jasper Johns exhibition. That was a book that I did very carefully, but I saw it as a catalog. I saw it as something that would be attached to the exhibition, would last two or three years, and would probably vanish, except for those people who collect catalogs from exhibitions. Instead the book was published in hardcover and was still in print 20 years later. I hadn't anticipated that. Art books, even in hardcover, don't last that long. Abrams, the publisher, then said at a certain point, "We would like to update that," and I was delighted to do that, because if this book was going to be around for so long, I really wanted it to be a different kind of book. I changed it quite a lot. But the first version of the Jasper Johns catalog is actually an interesting book from my point of view, because I said a lot of things I believe about how to make fiction realistic. That version has now vanished, except for them that look for it.

F: Is it nervous-making to know it's not possible for you to write anything disposable anymore, that every scrap will last?

MC: No, I think it's a joke. It's something that goes along with celebrity, I guess. The trick is to keep quality. I feel that I can continue to try hard.

F: What was the first book that made you think about becoming a writer?

MC: The first book was *A Study in Scarlet.* That was the first novel I can remember reading and saying, "Oh, I want to read more of this person."

F: Do you think you might start collecting Conan Doyle?

MC: It's still early.

F: Do you have a lot of books?

MC: They're just everywhere. It's very difficult, actually. Whenever there's any kind of an office move, 70 percent of the actual volume of the physical objects that I own is books.

TECHNOLOGY

F: Do you see yourself doing more electronic books, like the Voyager edition of *Jurassic Park*?

MC: I think that that's coming. I did a computer book in 1982, *Electronic Life*—it's one of my rarities—and I said people would be reading off of paper for another 20 years. And my editor at that time said, "That's an outrageous statement," but I think it's actually fairly accurate. I think a lot of ordinary reading will shift, too, not to video screens, because that's unpleasant, but to liquid-crystal, or these passive displays. If you can have a screen be bright enough that you can use it in daylight, then this way of reading will become more common. But I don't think they'll replace books at all.

F: Will technology change the way you write?

MC: No. On the one hand, I like books a lot. But I've always said there are several advantages to electronic books. For one, I'm always trying to search for some text, which is quite difficult in a book. The other thing is, I'm one of those people who, if people want to lend me books, I say "Don't, I'll go out and buy them," because I mark up books. Then I'm always, some years later, trying to decipher my handwriting. When I go on vacation I have this suitcase full of books, because I don't know what I'm going to want to read. And I do sometimes get resentful and think, if I had all that bulk on a few discs, I'd have more choices.

F: Where did the name for your first pseudonym, John Lange, come from?

MC: Andrew Lange is the author of fairy tales, and John is my first name. I saw these books as fairy tales, in a James Bond kind of way.

F: Where do you get your epigraphs?

MC: I think it originally comes out of an interest in doing nonfiction. There's more of that tendency to put epigraphs in front of chapters in nonfiction. I was trying to make it, especially in something like *The Andromeda Strain*, like nonfiction.

F: What about the sequel to *Travels* that was announced a while back?

MC: You know, I keep trying to get it done. In a few years, it'll happen.

F: Where does the name of your company, Constant C Productions, come from?

MC: It's the speed of light, as in e=mc squared.

F: How about the name of the corporation you used to copyright your early work, Centesis?

MC: Centesis is a medical term that means to puncture or deflate.

F: In the Eighties your career seemed to go into eclipse. Do you have a way of explaining that to yourself?

MC: Yeah, I do. I think that when you locate yourself inside the culture, vis a vis the ongoing technological situation, that you can fall behind. In my case, I think that I got ahead. Things like *Looker* were really about digital transformations. That technology, in fact, was used in 1993 for *Jurassic Park*, and it is only now, when we see Humphrey Bogart selling Diet Coke, that people are really starting to say, "Wait a minute, is there a problem about this?" So that was too far ahead. And even *Runaway*, which is about smart technology and robotic troubles in the texture of society, we had these sort of Newtons people were holding in the police department. I used to go to the screenings and the people would laugh. It was just too soon.

F: Do you ever censor yourself now, so as not to come down too far ahead of the curve?

MC: There are certain things that are very difficult to talk about. It's very difficult to tell a fish that the fish is in water. When I look at those movies, not only do I think they're addressing issues that seem too far ahead, they're also, in a way, ahead of me. There's a certain way that what I'm doing now is related to my life, and that's always been true. In *Airframe* it's something about what it's really like to be confronted with the media. There's a way in which I know that book comes out of my experiences. In the Eighties, the books didn't come out of experience.

F: Are the young protagonists in your work lately the result of your recent fatherhood?

MC: That's part of it. And also I think it really started with *Jurassic Park*, because I felt that you had to have more representation of the child's interest in dinosaurs. I was amazed at first. The first time I knew about it was when a friend of mine had an eight-year-old girl who was reading it. That was the first time I knew that very young children read *Jurassic Park*. They use it to teach science in schools. When I did *Lost World*, I actually contacted teachers and said, "I'm going to be doing the sequel, what subject areas do you want me to touch on? What are you having trouble with?"

F: I know you'd rather not talk about what you're working on next, but when can we expect it?

MC: I'm pretty sure it's going to be next year.

F: There's been a running discussion in Firsts about the 1993 gift edition of *Jurassic Park*. . . .

MC: It was signed with an autopen. I was certainly aware that was being done. When the controversy started, my reaction was, "Yeah, these people are completely justified." I mean, what were we thinking of? That isn't the right thing to do. I think the publishers were treating the signature as a sort of design element or something. And we were all kind of . . . caught.

F: Do you think people will collect you in 100 years the way they collect Jules Verne now?

MC: I have no idea.

F: Do you still do in-store appearances?

MC: The publishers wanted to do some for *Airframe*, so I did them in several cities, which was really interesting. It was a curious thing. The noontime ones were almost entirely book collectors, people who do all authors. Whatever author's in town, they go and get him. It had this very weird, impersonal quality. The ones that I did in the evenings were people who really wanted to meet me, and also a lot of kids. I liked the experience of talking to people who for one reason or another were interested in my books, and it was kind of spooky to realize that, at other times, I was signing books for people who didn't know who I was: "This week, Crichton, next week. . . ."

CHAPTER 2

Crichton's Books

READINGS ON
MICHAEL CRICHTON

The Terminal Man's Fascinating Technology and Solid Plotting Are Marred by Poor Character Development

Theodore Sturgeon

Famed science fiction author Theodore Sturgeon praises Michael Crichton for the many levels of expertise that shape *The Terminal Man*—including psychiatry, medicine, computer technology, and police procedure. He is impressed with Crichton's use of verisimilitude—a literary device that makes fiction seem more believable by use of specific, realistic details. However, Sturgeon writes that the novel falls short of greatness due to Crichton's failure to create sympathetic characters or an original ending. Harry Benson, the book's main character, is so difficult to get to know, and impossible to care about, that *The Terminal Man* becomes mere entertainment, when it could have been a careful work of art.

Michael Crichton operates from the very heart of an area called "verisimilitude." Comparisons with James Bond's adventures are inevitable; they remain, however, comparisons and not similarities. Dr. Crichton does not mention as many scientific advances as Ian Fleming does brand-names, and his priapic preoccupations are far, far less. Should Bond dynamite a tree, you just know it's going to fall precisely where he wants it; with a Crichton protagonist one is, happily, not quite so sure. Crichton's beat is in the interface between fact and invention, certainty and possibility, the established and the extrapolated. He shifts so expertly between these areas that a number of potential cavils become diluted, diffused—and defused.

The Terminal Man is a punning title, computer terminal being the second level. Or maybe the first. Harry Benson is the victim of a (fortunately, extremely rare) form of epilepsy involving the temporal lobe. His attacks take the form of blackouts plus terrible violence. The book is an account of a pioneering treatment, involving a microminiaturized computer powered by an atomic-energy source. Wired into the brain, the computer responds with countermeasures as the attack approaches—exact and controlled electric shocks to meticulously placed electrodes.

What is overlooked in the theories involved—electronics, medicine, psychology—makes the book. It is a factor at first intuited. It is then hypothesized. Finally, it is proved by the (svelte, sexy, compassionate, naturally) female psychologist—and, of course, by the patient, with the subsequent suspense, complete with threat and ticking clock, chase, capture, escape and confrontation.

Expertise Abounds

Crichton's work, here as in *The Andromeda Strain*, is crammed glossy-full with expertise: in medicine, psychiatry, administration, police procedure and especially computer technology. There is even a fine and fascinating bibliography—in which, by the way, I was most pleased to see a number of papers on the investigative technique known as stereotaxia. It is a method by which a surgeon, using a frame with three calibrated controls—one for each dimension—can precisely position a hair-thin probe anywhere in the brain, and by exciting it with a tiny electrical current, determine exactly which part commands which function.

To understand what cells control fingers and smiles is fascinating enough. When (as some researchers discovered) the current induced flashes of memory, sights, sounds, the possibilities become truly breathtaking. Some years ago a researcher told me that little was being done in stereotaxia any more, that funds had dried up. It is therefore good indeed to see that this work is continuing and has produced enough background research to be useful to Dr. Crichton in a fascinating book.

Such lures are tempered by purely novelistic considerations. Great fiction is never about things, or inventions, or even ideas—at least, not directly. It is the action and interaction of things and ideas on *people* that produce the memorable. If your protagonists are as hard to know, and as impossible to care about, as the victim Harry Benson; or as functionally predictable as a svelte woman doctor or the mad-scientist type who administers the hospital; and if your plotting, however chrome-plated, brings you to a totally tied-up happy ending with nothing left over, then you are left with only your ideation.

Dr. Crichton's verisimilitude locks itself to technology, not especially to living. (Science-fiction, with its own fences, hardly commits this any more. Nor do many new movies.) One regrets that so careful a piece of work should thereby remove itself from art into the area of entertainment.

Sphere Delivers Terror Through Precision Crafting

James M. Kahn

Sphere is a novel in which big leaps of imagination are made, writes James M. Kahn, but the reader eagerly tags along because Michael Crichton constructs his novel with great care and precision. Every detail of the novel's strange undersea setting is painstakingly presented so that the reader has complete faith in the reality of the fictional surroundings. From the growth rate of Pacific coral to the impossibility of making whipped cream while one thousand feet beneath the surface, the undersea world is made to seem completely real. When the book's leaps of imagination are made, the reader already has such faith in the reality of the book that all disbelief is suspended. *Sphere* also effectively echoes many elements of Jules Verne's *20,000 Leagues Under the Sea*, including the old-fashioned way the chapters are titled. Kahn is a physician and novelist whose books include *Timefall*.

An American sailing vessel laying phone cable in the remote Pacific runs into a snag. Navy exploration reveals, buried on a shelf 1,000 feet beneath the surface, what appears to be a gigantic spaceship—completely intact, showing no signs of corrosion . . . and at least 300 years old. Investigators flown to the scene include a biologist, an astrophysicist, a mathematician, and a psychologist. Startling questions arise from the very beginning: Is the craft alien or man-made? From our past, or from our future? And what is the nature of the mysterious hollow sphere they discover on board?

Crichton keeps us guessing at every turn, in his best work

James M. Kahn, "*Sphere*, by Michael Crichton," *Los Angeles Times*, July 12, 1987, p. 1. Copyright © 1987 by James M. Kahn. Reproduced by permission.

since *The Andromeda Strain*. Each chapter end reveals some new clue or poses some new threat that compels the reader to read on. And each new twist builds the pace with careful precision.

Precision is, in fact, a Crichton hallmark. His works give a sense of meticulous researching—no surprise, coming from a research MD. In *Sphere*, his details range from integral (The age of the space vehicle is dated by its coral growth: "Pacific coral grows two centimeters a year . . .") to casual (In a habitat 1,000 feet underwater—30 atmospheres of pressure—you can't make whipped cream: "Won't whip").

ENVIRONMENT OF BELIEVABILITY

But such digressions are not merely entertaining in science fiction of this sort. They are essential to establishing an environment of believability, so that when the inevitable speculative leaps *are* made (and there are a couple big ones here), the reader eagerly tags along. Somehow it's easier to buy the concept of *extraterrestrial* intelligence from an author who shows a little terrestrial intelligence himself.

Crichton shows plenty. Philosophical discussions abound, covering theories of extraplanetary life, black holes, human knowledge and behavior. The latter is actually a recurring theme, explored from the point of view of psychological Norman Johnson—the man who chose the other mission specialists, yet who remains under constant attack by them for being a champion of the "soft science" of psychology, in the face of their death-struggle against the considerably "harder" forces of inexplicable deep-sea monsters.

This whole set-up invites comparison to *The Andromeda Strain*—in which another group of scientists, cloistered in another isolated deathtrap, confront an extraterrestrial virus. Crichton himself raises the memory of that encounter early on in *Sphere*: "The fears unleashed by contact with a new life form are not understood. . . . But the most likely consequence . . . is absolute terror."

Terror—the terror of death, and of the essentially un-knowable—is at the core of this book. Terror, and how to confront it. "Understanding is a delaying tactic," muses mission psychologist Johnson. "Only people who are afraid of the water want to understand it. Other people jump in and get wet." So Crichton's academic credentials may be impeccable—but only in letting them lapse does his researcher become a hero in this tale.

There are more than sonar echoes of Verne's *20,000 Leagues Under the Sea* here—and that's another charm of the novel. One of the subliminal ways Crichton achieves this is by titling every chapter ("The Monster," "Beyond Pluto," etc.)—a literary device that is rather out of fashion, and rather evocative of all those grand adventure yarns we read as kids. And, not incidentally, rather effective.

There are some problems with the book: Crichton's dialogue tends to be a bit stilted at times, his characters a bit broad (there is the self-hating feminist; there is the weapon-mongering military man)—but these criticisms seem, at the end, pale in context, the context being that Crichton is a storyteller, and a damned good one.

What Makes *Jurassic Park* So Suspenseful

Elizabeth A. Trembley

Jurassic Park is by far Michael Crichton's most popular and successful book. As Elizabeth A. Trembley explains, Crichton builds and maintains a nail-biting level of suspense by separating the main characters, then constantly shifting the focus from group to group. Suspense is also generated by the various conflicts that drive the plot: humans versus nature, and the individual versus society. *Jurassic Park* draws from traditions established in classic science fiction and gothic literature, as well as classic horror cinema. The book shares similarities with *Frankenstein* and *Godzilla*, each of which features creatures powered by an awesome, unpredictable force: electricity, radioactivity, and, in the case of *Jurassic Park*, biotechnology. Trembley is the author of *Michael Crichton: A Critical Companion*.

Jurassic Park's plot makes it a novel readers find impossible to put down. In its numerous episodes, relation of cause and effect, suspense, and conflict, the novel presents a series of events that continually engage our interest anew.

Plots developed on the episodic pattern so familiar to popular literature present authors with a major problem. How does an author generate a series of harrowing situations for the main characters without creating a ridiculously unrealistic story line? Crichton avoids this potential pitfall by rotating the focus of his chapters among the main characters, who spend much of the book separated from each other. This rotation allows Crichton to generate frequent excitement without unrealistically having the same group encounter a climax in each chapter. The parade of short, exciting episodes becomes all the more thrilling because Crichton constructs them believably.

Crichton further produces a gripping plot by carefully constructing cause and effect. His straightforward, almost cinematic presentation clearly indicates how one mishap or judgment in error leads to another. Mathematician Ian Malcolm's constant lecturing on chaos theory reinforces this structure. Even the unpredictable is predicted, in fact *caused*, by the attempts to control the environment at the park. Malcolm knows that humans cannot control life's inherent unpredictability. Therefore, he foresees the failure of the systems that control the island even before they are built. Malcolm's statements to the others set the stage for the book's events. The disasters build one upon the other as parts of Malcolm's chaos theory.

In addition to containing tightly woven events, the plot's structure helps build suspense, most notably in the opening of the book. Crichton presents several episodes that seem only loosely connected to the main plot. But they are essential to developing a suspenseful grip on the reader through dramatic irony. This is a situation in which a reader knows more than the central character. The book opens with vivid depictions of strange lizard-like creatures mauling children. These episodes firmly establish our awareness of the animals' horrible destructive potential and create suspense as we await the next attack on an innocent victim. Readers remember these detached episodes as they encounter Jurassic Park for the first time. The bloody bodies contrast strongly with the peaceful sight of a giant apatosaur gently trumpeting in the distance. Though heroes Alan Grant and Ellie Sattler stand entranced, we know that violence threatens everyone on the island. The dramatic irony increases our tension and keeps us turning pages in suspense.

Development of suspense also requires readers' interest in

the conflicts that shape the plot. In *Jurassic Park*, two central conflicts create the disasters from which our heroes must escape. First is the conflict of human beings versus the natural order, one seen many times throughout the book. The most important example occurs when John Hammond and his bioengineering staff genetically engineer live dinosaurs. The genetic engineers, led by Dr. Henry Wu, attempt to alter the natural behaviors of these animals. For instance, they create only females so that the animals cannot reproduce. They make the dinosaurs dependent on lysine, so that if an animal leaves the boundaries of the park, it will die. Wu and Hammond fail to see the dinosaurs as wild creatures that will follow their instincts to reproduce, migrate, and survive: Instead they view the dinosaurs as amusements that can be controlled by fencing and hidden cameras. Nature, however, even when reconstructed by humans, does not so easily submit to human control. Eventually the dinosaurs' instincts overcome every containment. Then the humans must flee the unleashed power of the carnivorous giants they constructed.

The second major conflict of *Jurassic Park* involves the individual versus society. This is most prominent when an individual's self-interest conflicts with consideration for others. Each time someone chooses self-interest over the welfare of others, the situation at Jurassic Park becomes worse. Perhaps the most striking example of this conflict is seen in John Hammond's attempts to convince his investors that the park is safe. In a display of complete confidence, Hammond brings his small grandchildren to the island, placing them in terrible danger. Others make similar mistakes. Henry Wu brings the dinosaurs to life but remains ignorant of their abilities to escape, hunt, and reproduce. When computer programmer Dennis Nedry shuts down the security systems to steal materials from the labs, he lets loose the dinosaurs which kill him and others. Ed Regis abandons the children in the face of a tyrannosaurus attack—twice. This prevents their return to the control rooms, where only they can save the others.

However, when individuals choose to risk their own self-interest for the good of others, ultimately they also benefit. Alan Grant gives up his chance to escape the roaming dinosaurs when he opts to help the children. Ultimately this saves not only his own life, but the lives of all the survivors. Only the children can turn on the park's computerized power and security systems. Ellie Sattler volunteers to distract the velociraptors so that others can run between buildings and restore power to the computers. This not only helps the children's efforts, but grants Ellie the most exhilarating self-fulfillment of her life. Donald Gennaro's decision to risk his own life when rescuing others teaches him the relative valuelessness of money and prestige. . . .

GENERIC CONVENTIONS

Crichton consciously develops his work from the literary heritage of his chosen genre. *Jurassic Park* draws primarily on gothic and science fiction traditions. It also has similarities to classics of horror cinema. The novel closely resembles *Frankenstein*. Mary Shelley's classic work was the first novel to blend the horror and emotional intensity of gothic with the detail and presumed rationality of science. *Jurassic Park* follows in this classic novel's footsteps. Most gothic fiction focuses on the return of something dead or at least buried (for instance, Frankenstein's monster, vampires, werewolves, ghosts, dinosaurs). Often a long-hidden supernatural being brings complete disaster by revealing the true nature of itself and of the people with whom it comes in contact. Ironically, the *supernatural* being often proves more *natural*—or true to itself—than the other characters. In *Jurasssic Park*, for example, the existence of the dinosaurs is engineered by misguided men enslaved by the desire or need for wealth. However, the dinosaurs turn out to be creatures with personalities and wills of their own. As in *Frankenstein*, the human scientists try to create life, but fail to prepare adequately for their success. Though living creatures are naturally willful and independent, the scientists expect to create easily controllable automatons. When the scientists do succeed in creating life, disaster strikes because of their failure to acknowledge the creatures' uncontrollable instincts.

Science fiction delivers similar messages about scientists who disrupt the realm of nature. But it also adds other important conventions. *Jurassic Park*, like classic science fiction, taps into popular fears by relying on a realistic depiction of contemporary science. "All great science fiction must be science first and fiction second. Even more, it must tap into the reigning scientific paradigm of its era. For Mary Shelley's *Frankenstein*, that paradigm was electricity. . . . For *Godzilla*, it was radioactivity and the Bomb. For *Jurassic Park*, it is biotechnology" [writes Sharon Begley]. And that paradigm, or theme, must be depicted with solid believability, for that is the "hidden persuader" of all science fiction.

Crichton's novel does not suggest that science itself is wicked. But it does point out that poor judgment by scientists has created [what has been described as] "worrisome trends in a dramatic, potentially harmful, but correctable enterprise." The scientists depicted in science fiction often are not evil, but clearly have "more skill than wisdom" [according to John Skow]. In H.G. Wells's *The Island of Dr. Moreau*, the scientist pieces together new creatures from men and animals. Similarly, the Jurassic Park developers piece together dinosaurs from ancient and modern DNA. These are stunning feats of technical expertise, but are they good ideas? Once the technological challenge is met, the scientists are faced with responsibilities toward their creations. Here they fail. *Jurassic Park* explores "the doom that humankind faces if scientists are not diverted from their immoral and calamitous path" [Andrew Skolnick states]. Despite their strongest efforts, they cannot control nature. "It is man's utter incapacity to change nature that he [Crichton] finds so horrifyingly exciting, and that is the real thrill of *Jurassic Park*" [Vanessa Place].

Popular film has also influenced the presentation of *Juras-*

sic Park. King Kong and *Godzilla* typify movies that depict an ancient beast set loose in the modern world. The film version of Arthur Conan Doyle's *The Lost World* shows modern people who return to an ancient world. *The Birds, Jaws,* and other monster movies show animals attacking humans. And *The Blob* and *War of the Worlds* show the escalating power of unfamiliar creatures and the dangers they bring to humans. Crichton's childhood love of film and his professional success with film adaptations of his books no doubt influenced *Jurassic Park.*

Shadow World

George F. Will

Conservative commentator George F. Will, a longtime
Newsweek columnist and former editor of the *National
Review* criticizes *Rising Sun* for its negative portrayals of
both the Japanese and Americans. Crichton exaggerates
the Japanese influence in America while characterizing
Americans as lazy and therefore deserving of foreign domination. Due to its reliance on simplistic overgeneraliza-
tions, the novel is boring.

Popular fiction can popularize ideas, so Michael Crichton's
best-selling *Rising Sun* is dismaying as a symptom and repre-
hensible as an act. It is a crime novel well-stocked with murder and other mayhem—or, as Crichton says, other Japanese
business practices. It overflows with anti-Japanese passion, a
peculiar blend of fear and loathing and admiration.

Oliver Stone should make the movie of *Rising Sun*. Stone's
JFK preached that if you pierce the veil of reality, you will un-
mask a mighty conspiracy controlling America. But Stone
sees a made-in-America conspiracy. Crichton is selling an import. Listen to Crichton's fictional hero, an American initi-
ated into the mysteries of Japanese: "You must understand,
there is a shadow world here in Los Angeles, in Honolulu, in
New York. We live in our regular American world, walking
through our American streets, and we never notice that right
alongside our world is a second world. Very discreet, very private. Perhaps in New York you will see Japanese businessmen
walk through an unmarked door, and catch a glimpse of a
club behind. Perhaps you will hear of a small sushi bar in Los

Angeles that charges twelve hundred dollars a person, Tokyo prices. . . . They are part of the shadow world, available only to the Japanese."

All that is missing from Crichton's nightmare is a Japanese version of the *Protocols of the Elders of Zion*. The dark heart of the matter is that *Rising Sun* is not a harmless cartoon. We have seen such stuff before, with Jews treated as the Japanese now are. In *The New York Review of Books*, Ian Buruma demonstrates striking similarities between *Rising Sun* and the Nazis' infamous film *Jew Suss*. The film's attitude toward Jews is an ugly alloy of awe and rage: Jews—all of them; there is no individuality—are an inscrutable, clever, devious, dominating, inhumanly patient and implacably secretive people. They wield power behind impenetrable mists of subterfuge, manipulating the media and financial institutions and controlling, like marionettes on strings of money, corrupted politicians and pliable intellectuals.

This description fits Crichton's maniacally disciplined Japanese who exercise a Merlin-like mastery of the minutest details of their blueprint for domination. Crichton, speaking through his fictional wise man, drains his description of disapproval by adopting the languid relativism of sophomore sophisticates who say cultures cannot be good or bad, they just are. But Crichton is not bashful about one judgment: he despises contemporary America. *Rising Sun* fits the Zeitgeist because it is part of the literature of victimhood: But it portrays an America that deserves to be victimized, a nation sliding into Third World decrepitude because Americans are lazy incompetents.

Crichton's hero says Americans "don't make things anymore." Tell that to Boeing, Microsoft, Hewlett-Packard, Intel and thousands of other manufacturers (manufacturing is as large a percentage of [gross national product] as it was 20 years ago) responsible for American exports surging much faster than Japan's. Crichton's hero says Americans "don't work very hard." Oh? In the 1980s, population increased 10 percent, but the number of people employed increased 20 percent, to a labor force participation rate never exceeded, not even during World War II.

TO "WAKE UP" AMERICA?

In his cavalier assertions Crichton resembles Stone, the high priest of painfully earnest, oh-so-public-spirited paranoia. *JFK* is full of falsehoods that Stone's apologists deem justified for the Higher Good of awakening America from fatal slumber. Crichton says he wrote his novel "to make America wake up." It may work. No one can slumber while laughing at statements like these in the novel:

> "I guess by now they have seventy, seventy-five percent of downtown Los Angeles." "Hell, they own Hawaii, ninety percent of Honolulu. . ." (Wrong numbers and nouns. Japanese own 45 percent of prime commercial space in central Los Angeles and 90 percent of luxury-hotel properties in Honolulu. The British—perfidious Albion—own more in America than Japanese do, and foreign investment—which is not a bad thing—may have been proportionally as large a part of the nation's economy 80 years ago.) It is just not true that "the Japanese spend half a billion a year in Washington"; or that "nobody in Japan will buy American beef. If Americans send beef it will rot on the docks"; or that "most expensive American stores" would "go out of business without visitors from Tokyo"; or that "if a Japanese bought an American car, he got audited by the government"; or that "America has done nothing" in 20 years to lower the energy cost of finished goods; or that Japanese own "100 percent of Hawaii's Kona Coast"; or that America is "a poor country"; or that "the American economy is collapsing"; and so on and on and on. Didactic fiction is usually tiresome; this is insufferable.

Crichton's hero says he has been over into the future and it works: "Everything works in Japan." Crichton's problem is less that he is silly about Japan than that he is wrong about human arrangements generally. He should write less fiction until he has read more history. No society ever has been or will be the marvel that Crichton says Japan is. As for his wholesale extrapolation into the future of Japan's recent successes: Someone—[George] Orwell, I think—said that intellectuals tend to assume that trends will go on forever, but that is like saying [that because] Rommel got to El Alamein so he will get to Cairo. He never got to Cairo.

Rising Sun, an intended thriller, is intensely boring because its Robo Villain—an entire race, caricatured lacks humanity and hence lacks human interest. Today, as Japan's economy sags and its stock market crashes, the strongest American feeling about Japan is not fear but Schadenfreude [—taking joy in the tragedies of others]. What Crichton and other swooners about Japan admire so inordinately is orderliness, but it is the tidiness of life lived within an old and homogenous tribe. The Japanese are an old people but a novice nation. They have an ancient culture but are new to, and not at ease with, the essentials of modernity—individualism, pluralism, heterogeneity. Much of the messiness of American life is not mere inefficiency, it is yeastiness. It is creative fermentation, part of the fecundity of freedom. For 216 years that has made America what it remains—the rising sun.

Rising Sun: Japan-Bashing for the Masses

Mike Tharp

Writing for *U.S. News & World Report*, Mike Tharp contends that Crichton's novel *Rising Sun* projects derogatory and racist attitudes toward the Japanese. Crichton relies on a group of "revisionist" experts to give his book a sense of scholarship. As a result, most scholars find *Rising Sun's* conclusions to be based upon outdated and misleading information.

Ruth Benedict never visited Japan, but her 1946 book, *The Chrysanthemum and the Sword*, is still regarded as one of the best works ever about Japanese society by a cultural anthropologist. Popular novelist Michael Crichton has also had minimal firsthand experience in Japan—he has never visited for more than 48 hours at a time. But in contrast to Benedict's thoughtful, nuanced study of the Japanese character, Crichton's best-selling thriller, *Rising Sun*, paints the Japanese in unflattering broad strokes that some Japanologists find very troubling. Like 1946, 1992 is a time of deep suspicion about the Japanese. But where Benedict's book worked as a postwar corrective for American fears, *Rising Sun* promises to fuel the already overheated engine of Japan bashing that may be contributing to a rash of anti-Japanese hate crimes.

Crichton's opinion of 123 million people and their society can best be summarized by the words of his character John Connor, a Los Angeles police detective who has lived in Japan, speaks Japanese and supposedly understands the cul-

Mike Tharp, "Popularizing Contempt," *U.S. News & World Report*, vol. 112, March 9, 1992, p. 50. Copyright © 1992 by U.S. News & World Report, LP. Reproduced by permission.

ture. "But my friends always ask me to remember that [the Japanese] are human beings first and Japanese second," Connor says. "Unfortunately, in my experience that is not always true." The book is larded with such sentiments. The Japanese are called "the most racist people on the planet," and Americans who speak up for Japan are labeled "Chrysanthemum Kissers" and equated with Nazi collaborators.

SOURCES OF SUSPICION

Like Benedict, Crichton relies on the works of others for his understanding of Japan. He has been most influenced by a group of writers called "the revisionists," which includes Clyde Prestowitz, Karel van Wolferen, Pat Choate, Chalmers Johnson and James Fallows. The mildest of these argue that Japan has been indulged and spared criticism for years, while the harshest view Japan as a rogue nation, operating under predatory and adversarial rules of social and economic behavior.

Crichton sides with the harsh wing. Asked if he was sounding a call to industrial and technological arms for America, he replies, "Absolutely." He believes that the "decorousness" of Japanese society, which avoids confrontation, along with Japanese financial muscle, has limited criticism of Japanese behavior. He thinks the U.S. government has been asleep at the switch in allowing Japanese investors to roam unrestricted in America. And he advocates managed trade with Japan. "We import optical drives and export rice," he says. "We're turning into a nation of farmers. If that means slamming a few doors [on Japan], hey, life goes on."

This could all be dismissed as a fiction writer's privilege, except that Crichton demands, through an afterword and bibliography, that the book be considered seriously as Japanology. Unfortunately, serious scholars of Japan find that the conclusions in *Rising Sun* far too often are based on outdated or misleading information about how the Japanese do business and conduct daily life. Crichton criticizes the now notorious keiretsu system of interlocking shareholdings among a handful of giant corporate groups, for example, without noting that keiretsu power has waned dramatically in recent years.

Furthermore, Japanologists take Crichton to task for failing to understand two fundamental points about Japan: that the country is constantly changing, adapting to market forces and new ideas, and that the Japanese genuinely don't want to be No. 1. Most Westerners who live in Japan discover that the Japanese are satisfied to remain a strong No. 2. Claremont University Prof. Peter Drucker, who has written several books on Japan, says the claims that the Japanese seek world domination are "nonsense." They have a tremendous inferiority complex, he argues, and simply want to be respected in the international community.

Rising Sun is climbing the best-seller lists at a time when anti-Japanese incidents are already on the rise, including the alleged racially motivated murder of a Japanese businessman in California. Ultimately, it is the debasing of Japanese character that will be most destructive to U.S.-Japan relations. Indeed, Yuri Morita, a manager with Fujitsu Ltd. in Tokyo, says that Crichton's thriller is worse than the usual Japan bashing: "It's a Japan-loathing book. It's different from books about the Nazis or the Russians that hate the system but are sympathetic to the people. This book just hates people who are Japanese."

Disclosure's Caricatured Characters and a Clunky Plot Derail a Potentially Effective Satire

Julie Connelly

Disclosure is Crichton's attempt to write a serious novel about reverse sexual harassment in the corporate setting. However, Julie Connelly contends the book is too poorly written to be taken seriously. The novel's characters are one-dimensional caricatures. Furthermore, the plot is plodding and predictable, with twists being telegraphed pages in advance. Due to its many flaws, the book borders on the comedic. Julie Connelly is an editor at *Fortune*.

Would that Michael Crichton's new thriller, *Disclosure* were a better book! Anyone who attempts to make you forget that you are trapped in the economy section of an airplane, knees scrunched up under your chin as you glumly anticipate the slumgullion that will be served in-flight, has an opportunity to do God's work. Unfortunately, Crichton muffs his chance.

The story of the head of manufacturing at a computer company who finds himself fending off his hot-to-trot female superior ("You always had a nice tush," she tells her prey. "Nice hard tush.") has received more than its allotted 15 minutes of fame. Women are outraged that Crichton should focus on something so atypical in the corporate environment as reverse sexual harassment. Only about 5% of harassment cases are brought against women accused of coming on to the

Julie Connelly, "A Bizarre Tale of Sex in the Office," *Fortune*, vol. 129, February 21, 1994, p. 108. Copyright © 1994 by Time Inc. Reproduced by permission.

lissome lads who work for them. But Crichton writes fiction, after all, and as he told the *New York Times*, he is not obliged to deal with typical situations.

True enough. But he also wants to have it both ways: The story quite deliberately caters to men tired of having women trash them as boors and boobs whose brains reside in their underdeveloped gonads. Then, tucked away on the last page is the author's pious, three-paragraph disclaimer that his novel "is not intended to deny the fact that the great majority of harassment claims are brought by women against men. On the contrary: The advantage of a role-reversal story is that it may enable us to examine aspects concealed by traditional responses and conventional rhetoric."

CARICATURE CHARACTERS

Not in this book, fella. The characters are caricatures, the twists in the story are telegraphed pages in advance, and the plot goes clankety-clank. Take our hero, Tom Sanders, "a handsome man with the easy manner of an athlete." He is running the Seattle division of DigiCom Computer in all but name and expects to be made vice president when a hush-hush merger goes through. How does he react when he is beaten out by the beautiful, blonde Meredith Johnson, who lacks the requisite technical background for the job but is the CEO's surrogate daughter? He's disappointed, of course, but not angry. No, never angry. "You know, Tom," says another character, "sometimes you're too reasonable for your own good."

Tom is also pretty stupid, agreeing to meet Meredith, with whom he'd once been romantically involved, in her office after business hours. As she reaches to pour him a glass of wine, he begins to notice that she's wearing neither bra nor pantyhose under her conservative navy-blue suit. He also observes that she's locked the door. It's not long before he's sputtering "I'm married," in hopes of cooling her ardor. Foolish boy.

Fortunately, in between her passes, Tom finds a moment to place a call to the head of product design to discuss a flaw in a disk drive. Then she starts kissing him again, and he drops his cellular phone. Don't lose sight of that phone, reader, you'll meet it again. Tom finally escapes her clutches, having just stopped short of all the way, but the next morning he finds Meredith has accused him of harassment and is having him transferred to a lesser job. That's when he decides to sue her.

As the plot develops, you begin to wonder whether Meredith doesn't have a little more on her mind than Tom's tush. The manufacture of an important product is going haywire, and no one can figure out why. It's essential to conceal this information from the folks who want to merge with DigiCom, lest they call the whole thing off. You don't have to be a genius to figure out where the two story lines are going to converge. But I'll give you a hint: It all hinges on Tom's very convenient memory and an elaborate virtual-reality setup.

LACKLUSTER SECONDARY CHARACTERS

The other characters are as one-dimensional as Meredith and Tom. Susan, Tom's wife, is a lawyer but keeps complaining that women are oppressed. She's also an inept housewife who "took Mondays off, to spend more time with the kids, but she was not good at managing the routine at home. As a result, there was often a crisis on Monday mornings." The chief financial officer, another woman, is "colorless, humorless, and tireless, her dedication to the company was legendary; she worked late every night and came in most weekends."

The men in this high-tech company don't fare too well, either, except that they get to wear better clothes. There's the slimy general counsel who nervously pats his Hugo Boss suits, the angry head of product design garbed in black Armani, and the imperial CEO who favors dark-blue Caracini threads. The perpetually rumpled Bill Gates, please take note.

In these ponderous 400 pages, Crichton rips off a true story and a serious corporate problem. But in stronger hands than his, the idea of reverse harassment could make for a wonderful satire. Personally, I've always yearned to be a sexual predator, a man-eating tigress roaming the halls of *Fortune*, swishing her tail. But what stays my furry paw from brushing the well-muscled thighs of the office stud muffins is the fear that one of them would blurt out, "But you're old enough to be my mother!" Of course, mothers look younger these days, but ridicule, Mr. Crichton, is what changes behavior.

Timeline Is the Laudable Product of a Great Craftsman—Not an Artist

David Klinghoffer

National Review senior editor David Klinghoffer writes that *Timeline* demonstrates Michael Crichton's keen ability to write quality "craft novels"—products not of an artist, but of a craftsman—which are often more effective than art novels. Great craft novels like Crichton's, despite rejection by a more highbrow readership, are worthy of praise. Three components are necessary to write an outstanding craft novel: mystery, twists, and a time lock—a narrative device employed by Hollywood screenwriters to heighten suspense. David Klinghoffer is the author of *The Lord Will Gather Me In* and *The Discovery of God: Abraham and the Birth of Monotheism*.

In the catacombs of a ruined 14th-century French monastery, a team of grad student archaeologists from Yale stumbles on something peculiar. It's a convex piece of glass that looks like it could have come from a pair of—wait a minute, yes that's exactly what it looks like, but it couldn't be—a pair of eyeglasses of a distinctly 20th-century design. It must be a joke. But what's this? In an alcove of the same underground necropolis, sealed since well before the modern era, the team finds a packet of documents, parchment covered in medieval languages, nothing surprising among them except for one item toward the middle of the bunch. On this parchment is scrawled a message in recognizably 20th-century English lan-

David Klinghoffer, "Clockwork," *National Review*, vol. 51, December 6, 1999, p. 68. Copyright © 1999 by National Review, Inc. Reproduced by permission.

guage and script. It says: "HELP ME. 4/7/1357."

Yes, it must surely be a joke. For the desperate plea was apparently written in the hand of their distinguished professor, Edward Johnston, leader of this dig, who at the moment is known to be in New Mexico conferring with the management of a high-tech company that's been financing the expedition.

The ink and this parchment, as well as the document itself, are soon subjected to carbon-dating. Their antiquity is confirmed. The message was written in A.D. 1357.

This occurs on page 100 of Michael Crichton's new novel, and anyone who reaches that page and doesn't want to carry on to the end—to find out how that odd eyeglass lens and eerie letter on parchment got into an ancient, sealed ruin—can only be one thing: He must be an art-novel snob, and woe to such a reader. As Crichton has proved in a series of deservedly huge-selling suspense novels starting with *The Andromeda Strain* and running on to *Congo, Sphere, Jurassic Park*, and the rest, he is not an artist but a craftsman. And there's much that should be said, but generally isn't, in favor of good, modest craft novels.

Such books are written by a variety of often very wealthy men, including Stephen King, Tom Clancy, and Robert Ludlum, who are typically sneered at by everybody who ever wrote a book review. But King, probably the most gifted of the craft novelists, is more effective at what he does than are most contemporary art novelists—John Updike or Joan Didion, or you name it—at what they do. I reached this conclusion one night as I read King's *The Shining*—the scariest book I ever experienced—around 1 A.M. by myself in a small house in a quiet suburb. Crichton isn't too far behind.

THREE KEYS FOR CRAFT NOVELS

What makes an outstanding craft novel? Three things. First, a mystery. In fact every good story is ultimately a mystery story. In the case of *Timeline*, we want to know how modern artifacts got into a medieval catacomb. That question is resolved in the first third of the book, and I can tell you the answer because another intriguing mystery soon takes its place as the force that drives the narrative.

Those Yale grad students—Marek, Kate, and Chris—follow Professor Johnston to New Mexico. There they discover that the mysterious high-tech company, ITC, run by a slightly sinister Bill Gatesian figure, has employed principles of quantum physics to send Johnston back to medieval France—precisely to the site in the Dordogne region where Johnston's team has been digging. The students must go back in time to rescue him.

In his Introduction, Crichton notes that, as of 1998, something called "quantum teleportation"—like faxing a three-dimensional object—had been accomplished at three separate laboratories around the world. Who knows if that's true? Who cares? Either way, he explains the technology credibly enough. It turns out that when you quantum-teleport an object, it moves not between two locations on earth but between two locations in parallel universes. The theory is that every event in history that could have gone another way produces a split in the fabric of existence, resulting in two distinct universes. So there's a universe where Hitler lost the Second World War, and another where he triumphed. Skeptical readers will just have to accept that a person can travel from one of these universes to another, and from one time in a given universe to a different time in a different universe. The new mystery becomes: What is it that ITC hopes to do with the technology—apart from imperiling the lives of innocent grad students by putting them in the way of rampaging medieval armies jousting for turf in northern France, as happens here?

Second, a craft story must have twists, and there are nifty ones in *Timeline*. Like when Marek, Kate, and Chris, on the ground in 1357, realize that some stranger is listening in on their conversations. These are being beamed back and forth at a distance through a gadget lodged in the ear that's not only a walkie-talkie but a super-fast translator of all languages spoken in the Middle Ages. The stranger, who means them harm, can understand modern English.

Third, a craft novel needs what screenwriters call a time lock, a narrative device such that if the protagonists fail to accomplish their goal by the final moment of a predetermined period of time, then all hell's going to break loose. Here, the lock is set at 37 hours. When that time has elapsed, the team must have picked up Professor Johnston and got back in their quantum-traveling machines; otherwise they won't be able to return to the 20th century ever again.

A COMPELLING ACCOMPLISHMENT

Writing a compelling craft novel is, in fact, a lot like writing a screenplay. And anyone who thinks that's a snap should give it a try. The flotsam of lame suspense movies that churn through theaters every Friday shows that even all the money and the prestige of Hollywood isn't sufficient to create a really suspenseful suspense film more than in one of fifteen or so cases.

Timeline isn't Crichton's best book—the exposition can be cheesy, and a made-up citation from a non-existent book called *The Hundred Years War in France* on page one basically gives away the ending. So skip page one. But to generate and sustain real suspense over 400 pages, as Crichton does, is an accomplishment that's a whole lot easier to describe than to duplicate.

Timeline: Seductive Ideas Undermined by a Formulaic Narrative

John Dugdale

John Dugdale is the deputy media editor of the *Guardian* and a contributor to the *Sunday Times*, both of which are British newspapers. He argues that *Timeline* contains interesting material on quantum physics and history. However, the novel ultimately degenerates into a tedious succession of chase and fight scenes.

Steven Spielberg once called Michael Crichton 'the high priest of the high concept', uncannily adept at identifying upcoming 'hot-button issues' summarisable in three words or fewer. Science run amok in *Jurassic Park*, which Spielberg turned into a record-breaking blockbuster. Japanese economic imperialism in *Rising Sun*. Reverse sexual harassment in *Disclosure*. Airline safety in *Airframe*. So you can see why Hollywood studios have reportedly responded to the twin subjects of his latest novel with less than their usual rapture. Quantum theory? Fourteenth-century France? You're kidding, Mike, right? Crichton could make things much easier for himself if he were prepared to concede that *Timeline* is about time travel, but this is specifically and seemingly perversely denied ('the technology has nothing to do with time travel'). Instead, there is much burbling about 'orthogonal multiverse coordinate change' and 'wormhole connections in quantum foam'. Only belatedly, on page 120, does he come up with an image concisely conveying the novel's central premise. ITC, a sinister cutting-edge science corporation sponsoring a reconstruction of two castles and a monastery in the Dordogne, has developed a way to 'fax' people into the past, by 'compressing the information for an entire human being'.

A technical cock-up has faxed Edward Johnston, the Yale professor heading the Dordogne project, into the medieval era by accident; so his team of research assistants is sent back to 1357 too on a temporal rescue mission. Mark Twain buffs will be reminded of his time-travel fantasy *A Connecticut Yankee in King Arthur's Court*. But *Timeline* also reworks Crichton's own *Westworld* and *Jurassic Park*, where the good guys similarly risk getting trapped or killed in an earlier era. In these novels, however, history is only a theme park, whereas here the students are suddenly hurled from their meticulous simulation of the Middle Ages into the real past.

By for once risking penning a novel juggling two periods, two locations and two highly complex themes, Crichton sets himself obvious problems. *Timeline* is an awkward generic hybrid, part historical fantasy, part techno-thriller, and necessarily doubles the weight of pedagogic roughage for which his books are notorious. Most of the first half of the book consists of expert Crichton-proxies giving greenhorn reader-proxies tutorials—first on France during the 100 Years' War, then on quantum theory, then on the nitty-gritty of medieval life.

WEDDED TO HOLLYWOOD VALUES

But when the novel proper at last gets under way, with the young Yale posse threatened by the mounted goons of rival warlords Oliver de Vannes and Arnaut de Cervole, you often find yourself wishing you were back in Mr. Crichton's history and science classes. For what is seductive in *Timeline* is the academic material: the beguiling quantum conjecture; the eager, absorbing contrasting of received preconceptions about some aspect of 14th-century culture, such as sword-fights or hygiene, with the reality; the set-piece touristic trips to a tournament, a monastery, a castle under siege.

What is far less satisfactory, surprisingly, is the action-adventure narrative. Crichton stuffs his historical section with endless fights and pursuits, more than fulfilling cinematic requirements. He must know that, while chase scenes may be sensational on screen (his enemy knights, if filmed, will be just as scary as the *Jurassic Park* raptors), they are unreadable on the page. Yet he turns much of *Timeline* into what amounts to a tiresome prose transcription of a lance-'em-up medieval video game. Just as Prof. Johnston is wary of the corporation that backs his historical project, so Crichton is increasingly ambivalent towards the industry that lucratively realises his dreams—there is a sense in his choice of subject-matter of cheeky audacity, of defying movieland's morons to simplify quantum physics. But *Timeline*'s second half shows that its earlier academic apparatus was only playing hard to get, that he remains wedded to Hollywood narrative values. You could infer that he sees formulaic entertainment as a way to smuggle difficult ideas into the mass mind. But you could also infer that, if he cut the chase scenes, he might have to develop non-cardboard characters and imagine grown-up relationships between them.

Prey Is Vintage Crichton with a Few Firsts

Ned Vizzini

Ned Vizzini writes that *Prey* is a book of firsts for Michael Crichton: It is Crichton's first book written from the first-person point of view; his first book that he states from the start is a cautionary tale; and his first book with dark overtones of the supernatural. It is also Crichton's first book that focuses on a domestic setting. Crichton does a good job of portraying American family life in the first half of the book, then switches to his real forte: creating a compelling technological crisis with a roller coaster of action scenes and plot twists.

Ned Vizzini is the author of *Teen Angst? Naah . . .*

Pretend for a moment that Michael Crichton weren't the author of the true Great American Novel, *Jurassic Park*, and one of a half-dozen of the world's most powerful storytellers. His latest, *Prey*, would still be compelling for pacing that destroys your television. As it is, it stands as a turning point in Crichton's career: a rare first-person narrative, the first time he has explicitly stated his intention to write a cautionary tale and the first time he has injected his work with real supernatural dread. Where he goes from here is anyone's guess; it'll probably be downhill, but it'll be a fun ride.

"As flesh as today's headlines," reads the blurb on *Prey*, and it is, sure: The book is about swarms of computer-programmed nano-robots that fly around the Nevada desert killing people, kind of like tiny Predator drones. The first few chapters take

Ned Vizzini, "*Prey*, by Michael Crichton," www.nypress.com, vol. 15, 2002. Copyright © 2002 by New York Press. Reproduced by permission.

more from *People* than *Popular Mechanics*, though, as Crichton does his best job yet sketching an American family. Jack Forman is an unemployed Silicon Valley software engineer (Crichton never tackled the Internet boom, but he does a fine job with the bust) adjusting to his new role as "househusband . . . full-time dad, whatever you want to call it—there is no good term for it." He has three kids he loves dearly and a bitch wife, Julia, who hates them. Julia works at Xymos Technology (subtlety in naming has never been Crichton's thing); she's worth more than Jack ever was and is helming a big medical imaging project.

Jack suspects that Julia is having an affair. Here, as in *Disclosure*, Crichton does a note-perfect job with marriage and sexual politics (there's no sex, though, which is too bad because that scene in *Disclosure* was hot). Jack is indecisive and plodding as his wife does more and more outrageous things— lying about voicemails, phoning Nevada on her cellphone, not coming home at night. A sister urges Jack to talk to a lawyer, but he just *considers* and watches baseball games as Julia builds her case against him. ("You are shutting me out and keeping me away from my children. . . . I'm a good mother, I balance a very demanding job with the needs of my family. . . . You are not supportive of me," he replays in his head.)

CRICHTON GOLD STANDARD

The Jack/Julia machinations are so compelling you're almost disappointed when Jack gets a call that he's needed to fix a software bug from Xymos and we fade from home life into that special brand of sci-fi that only Crichton can do. You know the story: a civilian who seems unqualified goes into an alien environment and proves himself to company superiors/army men against a fearsome technological foe. For the middle 200 pages of *Prey*, we get the Crichton gold standard: three pages of scene-setting action interspersed with a page of dropping knowledge about the real world. The action scenes run like butter; the details on the swarms in the desert ("a peculiar low, thrumming sound . . . like a heartbeat . . . swirling and glinting silver") are frightening, believable and rapid-fire, as you learn that the nanoparticles can reproduce, evolve by the hour, pick up new behaviors, communicate with each other and kill things. (They were initially programmed to act as cameras.) Only at the end of the narrative is adultery reintroduced, with Julia quite literally cheating on Jack *with her work.*

This is when *Prey* gets truly frightening. The codependence of man and machine has been explored by many authors, but Crichton adds tongue-kissing and stumbles into a grand statement: we already live with fucking machines. We might as well be fucking them.

Then, suddenly, the book's over and you want to read it again because you read it too fast the first time. Some critics have labeled *Prey*'s educational passages too dense. That's because they're dumb. In truth, the science in *Prey* is not as complex as that in *Jurassic Park*, but if you're scared by computers or shrivel at words like "recursion" and "distributed processing," you won't enjoy it. Then again, if you shrivel at words like "recursion" and "distributed processing," you're headed for poverty and death in this world.

These are the technologies that will shape the next 30 years. (If you're a computer geek, of course, *Prey* is manna from heaven—there's actual code in the book! Heh heh.)

STUMBLES

As a writer, separate from his abilities as a pacer, storyteller and TV/movie conceptual guy, Crichton stumbles in *Prey.* Many paragraphs do a fine job describing an emotional state, then end with a summary: "It gave me the creeps," etc. These missteps are especially disappointing, since any decent editor would have torched them, but then again, no editor is credited in *Prey*; if there were one, they surely would have fixed the five-page introduction, Crichton's worst yet, redeemed only by his deadpan "it is difficult to anticipate what the consequences might be" toward the end. Perhaps the author feels he doesn't need editing?

You can understand why. Look at the list of works in the front of *Prey* and you'll see several—*Sphere, The Andromeda Strain, JP*—Indisputable American Classics. Perhaps Crichton is being afflicted by the same hubris he writes about.

No matter. The classics are out there, and MC might have one more left in him. Heck, *Prey* might even be the one. We wouldn't know yet since there's no movie. Because Michael Crichton doesn't just write books; he writes books, sells them as movies, compels you to read the book after you see the movie and makes sure you decide the book was better. He's got that multimedia attack; he's got more vision and balls than anybody out there; he's 60, so hopefully we'll get a half-dozen more out of him before retirement.

If you buy *Prey*, you'll finish it in three days. You'll think about it when you're away from it. You'll see the movie and know it inside and out. You might even worry about it before you go to sleep. What more do you want?

Well, you could want Crichton to take the plunge and finally write that sweeping family/media/law/culture commentary he's capable of. With *Prey* you know it's inside him, swarming to get out.

CHAPTER 3

Crichton's Films

READINGS ON
MICHAEL CRICHTON

Crichton on Directing

Gary Arnold

In this feature, *Washington Post* writer Gary Arnold profiles Michael Crichton and interviews him about his experiences as a film director. Originally inspired by an Alfred Hitchcock film he saw when he was twelve, Crichton went on to direct such films as *The Andromeda Strain, Coma, Westworld,* and *The Great Train Robbery.* He explains that an effective director must maintain a clear idea of the finished film and guide the process toward that end. Additionally, Crichton discusses how the skills he learned in medical school helped him become a better director.

A first impression of Michael Crichton is bound to be dominated by his height. At 6 feet, 10 inches, Crichton is surely America's tallest feature film director, and his height must confer a certain authority on the set, especially among professions as traditionally undersized as actor and producer. Pictures from the set of his new movie *Coma* include one irresistible shot of Crichton in conference with producer Martin Ehrlichman, who seems to be standing in a hole.

Crichton imposes control in a casual, leisurely style during conversation, suggesting a pleasant consultation with a nice, if cagey, young doctor. He was, of course, headed for a medical career before being permanently diverted by the success of his popular fiction, which he began writing in college strictly for money, and by filmmaking, which he began in 1972 with a TV movie, *Pursuit,* based on one of his own books, *Binary.* He directed his first theatrical feature, *Westworld,* a year later.

Gary Arnold, "A New Height in Films; Michael Crichton on Directing; My Son, the Director," *The Washington Post*, February 26, 1978. Copyright © 1978 by Gary Arnold. Reproduced by permission.

Despite its success, three years elapsed before Crichton got another movie underway. In the interim, he has published three books, a critical appreciation of Jasper Johns and two novels, one of which, the Victorian caper story *The Great Train Robbery,* will become his next film. "I was always interested in movies," Crichton said. "That was the original thing. I imagined being somehow involved in making movies long before I thought of becoming a doctor. Medicine never had the same fascination. When I was an undergraduate at Harvard, anthropology interested me more than any other subject. I wasn't emotionally committed to medicine. I entered medical school because I decided that being a doctor would be an interesting job.

A WONDERFUL, INTOXICATING WORLD

"I remember wanting to be a writer when I was a kid, but that got sidetracked in college. Although I was doing fast, cheap mystery novels for a paperback publisher, I wasn't thinking of writing as a serious, full-time profession. The greatest experience of my childhood was being taken to my first Hitchcock film, *To Catch a Thief.* I realize I was slow to discover this phenomenon. I'd led a rather isolated life as far as movies were concerned. That was 1954, and I was already 12. Still, late or not, it was an eye-opener. I discovered that there was this wonderful, intoxicating world up there. And out there.

"I started asking around and found out that this Alfred Hitchcock, the person responsible for this magic, was someone well-known. As a matter of fact, he did this sort of thing all the time. He even did it for a living. I'm not sure I've ever been the same since. Anyway, *To Catch a Thief* was the key. I doubt if we could presume to reproduce that sort of glamorous stimulation anymore. Where are the personalities to carry it? I don't quite see Robert De Niro supplanting Cary Grant."

Crichton's first exposure to a movie set occurred in 1967. "I was visiting friends in Los Angeles," he said, "and arranged to fulfil my dream of watching an actual Hollywood movie actually being made. Do you remember *Ice Station Zebra?* That was the one. It was an unforgettable experience. Here was this vast stage at MGM made up to resemble the Arctic or Antarctic. Anyway a huge artificial landscape of ice and snow, all brilliantly illuminated. And nobody was doing anything. There were these hundreds of people, actors and technicians and whatever, all waiting, waiting, waiting. Nothing ever happened while I was there. Maybe nothing ever did happen."

MAKING *THE ANDROMEDA STRAIN*

Crichton was still in medical school at Harvard when his science-fiction thriller, *The Andromeda Strain*, became a sensational best-seller. It was also the first book he had published under his own name. His mystery-writing pseudonyms were John Lange and Jeffery Hudson. Instead of interning, Crichton accepted a one-year research fellowship at the Salk Institute in La Jolla, California. Robert Wise's movie version of *The Andromeda Strain* went into production at Universal Studios while Crichton was still on his fellowship.

"I'd take every opportunity to drive up and watch the shooting," Crichton recalled. "It was a pretty big deal at the time. It was a $6-million movie, which seemed awfully expensive in 1970, when the business was in a slump, and the studio was constructing a lot of elaborate sets. Bob Wise was very considerate and helpful. He let me hang around and soak up what I could. At the same time I was going to parties around town, where I'd invariably meet actors and get acquainted. Not quite consciously I began to file away things I learned at these social occasions, especially the behavior patterns of actors and the kinds of complaints they most often express about directors.

"The thing about directing is that it looked do-able. It wasn't like undertaking brain surgery. You're surrounded by a sophisticated technology, but it doesn't need to be intimidating. There are trained specialists ready to help you, and I think every honest director from Orson Welles down has admitted that you can acquire adequate technical familiarity with the filmmaking process in a few hours.

"What you can't acquire in a few hours or a hundred hours is unerring creative control. To be effective a director must be the person with the most detailed image of the finished film. What happens on any production is that everyone comes in with his own idea. The actors are making their movie, the cameraman is making his movie, the designer is making his movie. You're obliged not to be confused by all this input, not to forget what you had in mind. When you fail to control or resolve all those influences, the picture is going to be screwed up in some way. It will be unsteady. The tone will wobble."

MEDICAL TRAINING USEFUL IN FILMMAKING

Crichton believes that the study of medicine has been practically useful in his filmmaking career. "Absolutely. For one thing, if you're studying to be a doctor, you're always required to pick up new skills. You learn to manipulate some tool you've never used before or go through some process you've never observed. You get accustomed to concentrating on the way things work and building up a variety of skills. You're geared to assimilate new things.

"At the same time you become accustomed to seeing a lot of people and learning to assess them quickly. After a while it becomes second nature to diagnose people on the street. Every medical student has found himself, for instance, standing in line at the bank and suddenly recommending that the man ahead see his doctor, because you know by his color that something is wrong with his liver.

"It's a more complete, reliable process than intuition. Even if you're not obliged to anticipate illness, the training can still help you anticipate other problems. You sense when trouble is brewing and you acquire a knack for soothing tempers and keeping people happy."

Crichton was born in Chicago but grew up with his brother and two sisters in Roslyn, New York, after his father became the executive editor of *Advertising Age*. Asked if his mother approved of his dropping medicine for the movies, he said, "Of course not. Deep down we all know I'm throwing my life away. But then what's a mother for?"

PLANNING THE FUTURE

If all the ingredients jell, Crichton's next production might evolve into a caper melodrama as entertaining as *The Sting*. The romantic co-stars are Sean Connery and Lesley-Anne Down, who could give an appreciative director as much to conjure with as Cary Grant and Grace Kelly did in *To Catch a Thief*. Crichton's original novel reads like a scenario augmented by period details and digressions, most of which should disappear into "touches" and the settings. At any rate, *The Great Train Robbery* is scheduled to begin shooting in Ireland in April, and the proof of this material should be in the filming rather than the writing.

"I'll have Geoffrey Unsworth and his crew," Crichton said, "so I'll be in good hands. The schedule is very tight, though, for a movie requiring so much period work and physical action. We've got 10 weeks, working 6 days a week, so I'll have to push it. I don't know if the story will have a sense of urgency, but the production sure as hell will.

"The work of directing is a function of time. I had only 6 weeks on *Westworld* and 12 on *Coma*, and I think there's a marked improvement in my work because of that. I feel more comfortable about what I'm doing, and I'm getting better. Some people complain that *Coma* is too careful and restrained, but at this stage I can't be certain how justified the criticism is. I was hoping for a gradual acceleration of suspense. After holding back in the first half of the film, we try to break out in the second half. Even the music is concentrated in the second half. Before that there's nothing but source music.

"Maybe it's not a complete breakout, and it could be a feature of the way I am. In one sense I think I'm inclined to be a minimalist. I'd like to achieve effects with the least technique possible. I'm more likely to err on the under-shoot side of things. On the other hand I know I'm attracted to attempting more exciting effects. I suspect that attraction will grow stronger with each new movie."

Movies Cannot Be Scientifically Accurate

Michael Crichton

In this speech to the American Association for the Advancement of Science, Michael Crichton criticized the scientific community for their complaints about the portrayal of science and scientists in the media. He goes on to carefully explain that science cannot be accurately portrayed in the movies. Films like *Jurassic Park* are fantasies whose first priority is to tell a good story. In the process of doing so, scientific veracity must sometimes be sacrificed for the sake of the plot.

Scientists dislike negative portrayals of scientists and scientific research in the media. However, a closer examination reveals that these media images are inevitable and probably cannot be changed. Science should turn instead to practical steps to improve its image with the public.

I come before you today as someone who started life with degrees in physical anthropology and medicine; who then published research on endocrinology, and papers in the *New England Journal of Medicine*, and even in the *Proceedings of the Peabody Museum*. As someone who, after this promising beginning, turned to a life of crime, and spent the rest of his life in what is euphemistically called the entertainment business. And it is from the perspective of someone who has lived in both worlds that I want to speak to you today.

Scientists often complain to me that the media misunderstands their work. But I would suggest that in fact, the reality is just the opposite, and that it is science which misun-

Michael Crichton, speech to the American Association for the Advancement of Science, Anaheim, California, January 25, 1999. Copyright © 1999 by Michael Crichton. Reproduced by permission.

derstands media. I will talk about why popular fiction about science must necessarily be sensationalistic, inaccurate, and negative. I'll explain why it is impossible for the scientific method to be accurately portrayed in film. I will explain why I think traditional concerns about media are misplaced, and I'll suggest some steps that science can take to genuinely improve its image.

I'll speak informally, so I ask your indulgence if I refer to "science" as if it were something monolithic, or if I refer to mass media and popular culture interchangeably. In the past, I would have also have asked you to excuse me for talking about news and entertainment as if they were interchangeable—though, of course, these days they are.

But let me return to my original point: that science misunderstands media. Let's begin by talking about two recent and typical examples of this misapprehension. One is an essay in the journal *The Sciences*, and the other is an article from the *New York Times*.

MOVIE SCIENTISTS

This is from the November-December [1998] issue of the excellent journal *The Sciences*. The article is entitled "Script Doctors," and the subtitle reads "Movie Scientists, from evil doctors to the merely insane, from bumbling nerds to stalwart heroes, still inform public perceptions of the real thing." No, they don't.

Notice first how arbitrary the characterization is. The illustrations show an old version of *Dr. Jekyll and Mr. Hyde*, and a still from *Indiana Jones and the Temple of Doom*. But Stevenson's story isn't about science, it's about the dual nature of man. And Indiana Jones is not a figure that leaps to mind when we think of scientists in movies. He's an adventurer. And the film *The Temple of Doom* is, like *Gunga Din* before it, a story about a murderous religious cult. To identify these pictures as representations of scientists is a stretch.

Another page from the same article, which shows a nasty-looking fellow from a movie no one has ever seen, called *Re-animator*, based on an H.P. Lovecraft story. We also have Sharon Stone from a movie I co-produced, *Sphere*. You may not like the flawed character she plays—the reviewer doesn't—but why single her out, rather than Dustin Hoffman, or Sam Jackson, or Peter Coyote? Everybody in *Sphere* is a scientist. Do you expect them all to be admirably portrayed? If so, do you think that corresponds to real life?

SCIENTISTS HAVE FLAWS

I ask that because I sometimes think scientists really don't notice that their colleagues have flaws. But in my experience scientists are very human people: which means that some are troubled, deceitful, petty or vain. I know a scientist so forgetful he didn't notice he'd left his wife behind at the airport until the plane was in the air. I once was at a party with Jacques Monod when a gorgeous young woman—a Ph.D. bacteriologist—came up to him and said, "Oh, Dr. Monod, you are the most beautiful man in the room." And he *preened.* But why not? He *was* very handsome in a sort of Camus-existential-Gauloise-smoking way. We all know that Nobel Prizes tend to magnify human foibles, anyway.

I find these flaws reassuring, but an essay like this, which primarily focuses on negative rather than positive images, is a perennial exercise in self-flagellation, and is what I call ritual abuse. The implication is that scientists are singled out for negative portrayals, and that the public is therefore deceived in some way we should worry about. I say, that's nonsense.

Let's be clear: all professions look bad in the movies. And there's a good reason for this. Movies don't portray career paths, they conscript interesting lifestyles to serve a plot. So lawyers are all unscrupulous and doctors are all uncaring. Psychiatrists are all crazy, and politicians are all corrupt. All cops are psychopaths, and all businessmen are crooks. Even moviemakers come off badly: directors are megalomaniacs, actors are spoiled brats. Since all occupations are portrayed negatively, why expect scientists to be treated differently?

But wait, you may be thinking. Don't these movie images provide some insight into the attitudes of the wider society? Don't they reflect the society in some way? No, they do not: for proof of that, you need only look at images of women in the last 50 years. Fifty years ago, movies were characterized by strong women—Crawford and Stanwyck and Bette Davis. Women of intelligence and substance, women to be reckoned with. Since then, during a time of dramatic change for women in society, the movies have portrayed women primarily as giggling idiots or prostitutes.

So I suggest to you there is essentially no correspondence between social reality and movie reality. None at all. And hence no point in worrying about movie portrayals.

MOVIE IMAGES

Scientists are not alone in their concern about movie images. Other professions worry as well. Consider the 1994 essay by Victoria Beard, "Popular Culture and Professional Identity: Accountants in the Movies," or another by Phillip Bougen, "Joking Aside: The Serious Side to the Accountant Stereotype." Many professions aren't happy.

Here's a recent article from the *New York Times:* "Scientists seek a new movie role, hero not villain." Again, notice the arbitrary nature of that dichotomy. We see three pictures: Charlie Chaplin in *Modern Times*, a movie that is mentioned as critical of technology. Charlie Chaplin is run off his feet by racing technology. Imagine feeling that way! But of course it's a comedy. Next, *Jurassic Park*, where the caption reads, "Scientists as bunglers: Richard Attenborough, left, hatches a deadly dinosaur." But Richard Attenborough is not a scientist, he's a businessman. The other two people in the picture are scientists and they have had nothing to do with the bungling. Indeed, the scientist on the right is about to complain about the bungling, as any sensible person would. How does this story moment get encapsulated as "Scientists as bunglers"?

In passing, I'd remind you *Jurassic Park* does have a scientist as its hero. He's right there, Alan Grant. He saves the kids, he saves the day, rights the wrongs, and looks dashing. Beside him is another hero, Ellie Sattler, a botanist. So in a movie where nearly every character has a doctorate, why talk about wanting to be heroes not villains? The scientists already are heroes. Why are they so insistent on discounting the positive portrayals? Ritual abuse.

The third picture, from the movie *Contact*. The caption here is "Real science: Jodie Foster's driven search for extraterrestrial life won plaudits from astronomers." We all know what that means. That means some of the background is authentic, or some technical dialog is good, or the filmmakers went to Puerto Rico and filmed an actual radio telescope. But to call a movie about contact with extraterrestrial life an example of real science is very odd, indeed.

Let's move beyond the issue of images of scientists, because this discussion is really about something more interesting: how the scientific method is portrayed in fiction.

THE SCIENTIFIC METHOD

I've said that scientists don't understand media, and one form of misunderstanding concerns why stories about the scientific method are as they are. I hear four principal complaints:

Unnecessary Added Plot (sex, violence, explosions, etc.)

Inaccurate and Implausible Plot Devices

Fear-based and Negative

Why Not Show the Real Method?

Let's take these in order. Why are unnecessary razzle-dazzle and exaggerated plot elements meretriciously added? Well, because it's a movie. Movies tell larger-than-life, exaggerated stories. Most feature sex and violence and explosions whenever possible. As movie mogul Sam Goldwyn said, "Sex will outlive us all."

A variant complaint is to say the story doesn't need one or another element. Oxford biologist Richard Dawkins, whom I very much admire, is quoted as saying "the natural world is fascinating in its own right. It really doesn't need human drama to be fascinating." And he wondered why *Jurassic Park* had to have any people in it at all, when it already had dinosaurs.

Of course the natural world is fascinating in its own right, but *Jurassic Park* isn't the natural world. The jungle is on a soundstage at Universal. It has been built to suit the action; if an actor has to climb a tree, the fiberglass bark is supported inside with metal girders to hold the weight. It is lit by artificial light.

And for the most part, the dinosaurs aren't on this set at all: they're added later by computer. The dinosaurs are photo-realistic animations, exactly like Mickey Mouse, except with more pixels. Furthermore, it's not as if the dinosaurs had some inherent accuracy and the people are added fictions. It's all equally fictitious. No one knows what dinosaurs looked like or how they behaved. Technical advisors can't tell you, because no one knows. We have skeletal remains, some trackways, and some impressions of skin texture. But the minute you start adding muscles and skin color and movement and behavior, you're guessing. Therefore the film portrayal of dinosaurs is fantasy. A novelist imagined their behavior. Artists imagined their appearance. Their actions were honed, and repeatedly revised by artists at Industrial Light and Magic until they looked right to Steven Spielberg. There is nothing remotely real about them.

EDITED NATURE

But let's imagine, for a moment, that dinosaurs were real, and you could film a sort of Discovery Channel segment about them. Would that film be real? Are any of the nature films we see on television "real?" For the most part, no, because those films take raw footage, sometimes filmed over years, and cut it together to make a familiar narrative: the young cub goes on its own, meeting amusement and danger.

Mother protects and defends her cute babies. The male is banished from his harem and sulks. And so on. These stories frequently do not occur in front of the cameras. They occur in the editing room. Why are the films cut that way? Because people like stories. They find sequential narratives, even when palpably untrue, interesting and organizing. In fact when people go on safari to Africa they're disappointed to find the animals aren't acting out the little half-hour vignettes they've come to expect from TV. Alternatively, when they do find a real life episode, it often lasts too long: a dominance fight between hippos can go on for hours. With no convenient commercial breaks in which to change film and go to the bathroom.

But Dr. Dawkins said he didn't know why you needed the people in the story. The answer is that the person who dreamed up this particular fiction wanted it to be that way. It was written to revive the corny movies of people and dinosaurs together that I had loved in childhood. *King Kong, One Million Years BC*, all of that. *Jurassic Park* is meant to stand in a long line of related movies. It is thus explicitly a work of fiction. The natural world is entirely irrelevant.

COMPLAINTS OF INACCURACY

Let's go to the second point, inaccuracy and made-up plot devices. Scientists from Leo Szilard to Isaac Asimov to Carl Sagan have all written fiction—and all have unhesitatingly used inaccurate and gratuitous plot devices. There must be a reason. Carl invented a message, he invented a machine, and he invented an extraterrestrial life. None of this could be called accurate in any reasonable sense of the word. It's fantasy. Asimov is best known for his *I, Robot* series. No accuracy there.

In a story like *Jurassic Park*, to complain of inaccuracy is downright weird. Nobody can make a dinosaur. Therefore the story is a fantasy. How can accuracy have any meaning in a fantasy? It's like the reporters who asked me if I had visited genetic engineering firms while doing my research. Why would I? They don't know how to make a dinosaur.

But on another level of texture and detail, accuracy is always at risk, because it is never the most important value. Jack Horner, the paleontologist who served as the film's advisor, was dissatisfied with the portrayal of a dinosaur dig, where people are exposing bones. He'd gone to a lot of trouble to plan a real sequence for Steven, instead of the unrealistic one that was shot. I said, "Would your sequence take the same amount of time?" No, he said, it would take a little longer. Maybe another minute. "Well," I said, "there's your answer." Because a minute is a very long time in a movie. And the dinosaur dig isn't a plot point, it's only meant to establish a milieu for the characters. Verisimilitude in a narrative is more important than veracity.

SCIENCE BOOSTERISM

Point three. Why are the stories about science always so negative? We've already discussed that characters in every profession are shown negatively. But what about the stories themselves: why can't we have positive stories?

One answer is that people like scary movies. They enjoy being frightened. But the more important answer is that we live in a culture of relentless, round-the-clock boosterism for science and technology. With each new discovery and invention, the virtues are always oversold, the drawbacks understated. Who can forget the freely mobile society of the automobile, the friendly atom, the paperless office, the impending crisis of too much leisure time, or the era of universal education ushered in by television? We now hear the same utopian claims about the Internet. But everyone knows science and technology are inevitably a mixed blessing. How then will the fears, the concerns, the downside of technology be expressed? Because it has to appear somewhere. So it appears in movies, in stories—which I would argue is a good place for it to appear.

And let's remember there is genuine reason for concern.

As Paul Valery put it, "The whole question comes down to this: can the human mind master what the human mind has made?" That's the question that troubled Oppenheimer. It troubled the editors of the *Bulletin of the Atomic Scientists.* It troubles many scientists now. And it should.

Finally, our society is now dependent on technology, and dependent on science. With so much power, science will inevitably receive strong criticism. It comes with success. It's entirely appropriate. Take it as a compliment. And get over it.

THE SCIENTIFIC METHOD VERSUS MOVIE RULES

And so we come to point four. Why not show the real scientific method in stories?

The article quotes my friend David Milch, a creator of *NYPD Blue.* His answer is blunt: "The scientific method is antithetical to storytelling." And he's right, at least for movies. Movies are a special kind of storytelling, with their own requirements and rules. Here are four important ones:

Movie characters must be compelled to act

Movies need villains

Movie searches are dull

Movies must move

Unfortunately, the scientific method runs up against all four rules. In real life, scientists may compete, they may be driven—but they aren't forced to work. Yet movies work best when characters have no choice. That's why there is the long narrative tradition of contrived compulsion for scientists. In *Flash Gordon*, Dr. Zharkov must work or else Dale Arden will be fondled by Ming the Merciless. In countless other stories, the scientist was given a daughter, so she could be captured by the bad guys, to force the scientist to work. Another time-honored method to compel is to build in a clock. That's what I did in *The Andromeda Strain.* You must accomplish a task before something awful happens. Or you can murder the character's family, thus forcing him to track down the bad guys. But however you do it, the end result is always the same: the movie character is compelled to act.

You can dispute this rule, and you can find exceptions. But the great majority of dramatic movies work this way.

Second, the villain. Real scientists may be challenged by nature, but they aren't opposed by a human villain. Yet movies need a human personification of evil. You can't make one without distorting the truth of science.

Third, searches. Scientific work is often an extended search. But movies can't sustain a search, which is why they either run a parallel plotline, or more often, just cut the search short. There's a fabulous sequence in *The French Connection* where the cops spend all night tearing apart a car, searching for cocaine. But on film it only lasts about thirty seconds. Whereas if you short-circuit the search in science, you aren't faithful to the nature of research.

Fourth, the matter of physical action: movies must move. Movies are visual and external. But much of the action of science is internal and intellectual, with little to show in the way of physical activity. Even the settings of science are unsatisfactory: contemporary laboratories aren't physically active, like the bubbling reagents and lightning sparks of old Frankenstein.

For all these reasons, the scientific method presents genuine problems in film storytelling. I believe the problems are insoluble. The best you will ever get is a kind of caricature of the scientific process. Nor will the problems be solved by finding a more intelligent, dedicated or caring filmmaker. The problems lie with the limitations of film as a visual storytelling medium. You aren't going to beat it. And of course, movies are resistant to the advice of outsiders. As Sam Goldwyn said, "When I want your opinion, I'll give it to you."

Jurassic Park: Imagining Dinosaurs in the Modern World

Don Lessem

Don Lessem is the founder of the Dinosaur Society and author of *Dinosaurs Rediscovered*. He also cowrote *The Complete T. rex* and *Digging Up T. rex* with John R. Horner, the paleontologist who served as the principal adviser to Steven Spielberg during the filming of *Jurassic Park*. Horner is also the real-life model for *Jurassic Park*'s hero, Alan Grant.

Lessem provides a behind-the-scenes look at the filming of *Jurassic Park* and explains the great lengths Spielberg went to in order to ensure a realistic film. He scrutinizes the authenticity of the behavior and characteristics of the dinosaurs portrayed in the book and film. He also explores the feasibility of a real Jurassic Park, addressing the plausibility of bringing dinosaurs to life as well as outlining the requirements for housing dinosaurs in a zoo environment.

A keen-eyed, man-sized Velociraptor leaps out of the darkness to slash at its victim. A Triceratops lies on its side, waylaid by a meal of poisonous berries. Hot-blooded baby dinosaurs grow like wildfire in a computer-controlled hatchery. Ostrichlike dinosaurs sprint through the forest. And lurking ominously in the shadows is perhaps the greatest killing machine ever known to nature or the special-effects industry—a 40-foot-long Tyrannosaurus rex.

Welcome to the world of *Jurassic Park* and dinosaurs more

Don Lessem, "Designing Dinosaurs: How to Bring *Jurassic Park* to Life," *Omni*, vol. 15, July 1993, p. 50. Copyright © 1993 Omni Publications International, Ltd. Reproduced by permission.

alive than at any time in the last 65 million years.

"They're the best dinosaurs people have ever made, period," says John R. Horner, the Montana dinosaur paleontologist who was the film's principal adviser. Horner is also, in more respects than anyone alive, the true-life model for *Jurassic Park*'s hero, Alan Grant. Just how good are these dinosaurs?

I first met Velociraptor, the most villainous of *Jurassic Park*'s dinosaurs, in its least prepossessing posture, as a skin on a coat rack in the Los Angeles studio of special-effects expert Stan Winston *(Aliens, Terminator II)*. Still, I did a frightened double take at the sight of what looked like an animal hide looking back at me with an unnerving stare.

Never mind that re-creating Velociraptor and his kind took plenty of sculptors, hydraulics, and computers—a budget larger than all the dollars ever spent on dinosaur science— and Steven Spielberg's directorial savvy to make the rest of us suspend our disbelief. And ignore the fact that Michael Crichton's fantasy of dinosaurs reconstituted from fragments of their DNA locked in amber is just that—a fantastic feat of genetic engineering so far beyond present technology and scientific ethics that neither genetic researchers nor Crichton will contemplate its near-term prospects seriously.

Do *JURASSIC PARK*'S DINOSAURS ACT AUTHENTICALLY?

Instead, think about living with dinosaurs, with Velociraptors or Triceratops—as so many kids and paleontologists are happy to do. The fantasy is so compelling, the cinematic trickery so wizardly, that we really can imagine live dinosaurs in our world. But are the hot-blooded and often hot-tempered dinosaurs of *Jurassic Park* behaving as live dinosaurs would? If so, how could we keep ourselves safe from them, and them safe from us?

These questions were very much on the mind of Crichton as they were to Spielberg and a host of hired dinosaur guns— scientists, artists, and special-effects experts—during two years of elaborate preproduction, several months of shooting, and in the final generation of computer graphics in postproduction—all under the shroud of extreme secrecy. By hiding the dinosaurs in progress from the press (the models were even cloaked in sheets on the sets between scenes), Spielberg wasn't zealously guarding trade secrets as much as he was wishing to preserve what he calls their "magic"—keeping the media and public focus away from high-tech gadgetry and under the compelling illusion that living dinosaurs do exist, if only on celluloid.

As a writer on dinosaurs, I had several opportunities to visit with the dinosaurs and the director during the laborious process of bringing them to life. On each occasion, Spielberg was eager to talk dinosaurs. He wanted to know, did he have T. rex's proportions right? Dead right—though the arms were a bit long. What did they sound like? He asked that paleontologist David Weishampel send him tapes of simulated duckbill sounds.

The lengths to which the makers of *Jurassic Park* went in order to adhere to science fact and science possibility, not science fiction, were much in evidence during shooting of an opening scene of the film, where paleontologist Grant unearths two dinosaur skeletons from a Montana hillside. A badlands mound in a wilderness refuge in the Mojave Desert was outfitted to resemble a quarry. Horner's Museum of the Rockies and its dinosaur sculptor Matt Smith supplied the cast skeletons. The simulation extended to mounding fake rocks around the fossils since a genuine hole couldn't be dug on protected land. Horner sprinted from set to set, ensuring that the tools, the costumes, the dialogue, befit an actual excavation. When I mentioned a niggling error to Spielberg in Horner's absence—that actress Laura Dern was incorrectly referring to a dinosaur skeleton's death-rigor-curled pose as the product of "lots and lots of time"—the director called a halt to the shooting while Dern's lines were redrafted.

But ultimately, *Jurassic Park*, the movie, maintains greatest fidelity not to dinosaur science, but to *Jurassic Park*, the book. That book, as its author Michael Crichton freely admits, is at best reasonable speculation. "I imagined that a great deal was known about dinosaur behavior—what these animals looked like, what their coloration was, what their movements were, what their social life was like. In fact, there wasn't any information. There are only educated and not-so-well-educated guesses, and those have changed over time."

THE KNOWN TYRANNOSAURUS REX

We may never know what colors dinosaurs were, and they could have been polka-dotted as easily as decked out in the jungle-camouflage tones of the movie's creatures. What we do know and can reasonably speculate about dinosaurs is often, but not always, consonant with their image in *Jurassic Park*. For economic reasons, the cast of dinosaurs—a hodgepodge of animals that have more to do with the Cretaceous period (135 to 65 million years B.P.) than with the middle era of dinosaurs, the Jurassic period—has been reduced to just six.

Tyrannosaurus rex is the king of *Jurassic Park*, as it was in dinosaur times. In *Jurassic Park*, it's a vicious, fast-moving predator capable of crushing Ford Explorers and gripping prey with its prehensile tongue. T. rex's banana-sized teeth were capable of puncturing bone and so perhaps crunching metal, but tongues don't fossilize. "Some reptiles have sticky tongues, but I'd bet T. rex's tongue couldn't do all that," says James Farlow, a University of Indiana, Purdue, dinosaur paleontologist and T. rex authority.

Horner himself questions a far larger assumption about T. rex—that it was a savage hunter. In his new book, *The Complete T. rex*, he attacks the common perception of T. rex as a predator. "Most big meat eaters today are scavengers. Even the hunters get most of their food by scavenging. There were plenty of corpses around for T. rex to eat. There was no good reason for it to go chasing a lunch." And if it did as in *Jurassic Park*, Farlow points out, "T. rex would be pretty stupid to keep chasing these people—four lousy bites—when it could be getting a lot more meat out of one dinosaur in the park."

But another of Crichton's speculative T. rex behaviors met with general agreement from dinosaur scientists: T. rex would be particularly attracted to moving animals, although motionless prey wouldn't necessarily escape its ravages. "A lot of predators pick up on motion," says Farlow, "Toads, birds. It's not a bad guess for T. rex." There was logic, too, in the book's speculation that T. rex swam, as it did in a scene not adapted to the film, although the filmmakers did call to inquire if T. rex could swim. (The answer is probably yes—there are footprint marks pushing off a shore to suggest smaller carnivorous dinosaurs did swim, so T. rex may have also.)

DUBIOUS DINOSAURS

While dinosaur paleontologists agree with the portrayal of the gentle plant eaters of *Jurassic Park*, a cowlike Triceratops and a treetop-grazing Brachiosaurus, a few scientists—Farlow among them—say the small villains are based on fantasy, not fact. In the book, the tenfoot "spitter," a Dilophosaurus, fans its cobralike hood and spits poisonous venom. The real-life Dilophosaurus was nearly 20-feet long and, like all dinosaurs, left no clue of fans or poison glands.

Crichton explains how he made the fantastic leap. "We know there was this great variety of animals that at one time populated the earth, and they must have had an enormous variety of behaviors. I imagined some of them were poisonous and could spit as certain modern-day reptiles can." Farlow isn't persuaded. "Sure cobras spit, and anything's possible." According to some scientists, however, you can't get much farther apart than snakes and dinosaurs on the family tree of diapsids (the evolutionary group that includes animals best known as "reptiles").

No *Jurassic Park* dinosaur raises more questions among scientists than does its most dastardly dinosaur, Velociraptor. These raptors are as big as we are, considerably faster, and savvy and dexterous enough to turn a doorknob. Crichton featured the raptors with their size and smarts in mind. "You have certain obligations when casting dinosaurs—a Tyrannosaurus, a Stegosaurus, a Triceratops. Then you choose among the less-well-known animals that interest you."

According to Crichton, he was attracted in particular to Velociraptors four to six feet tall. "I imagine them to be very quick, very bright—bright as chimpanzees and more vicious," he says. "Compared to body size, they had a larger brain case and so they were more likely to be intelligent, quick moving."

Crichton speculates that Velociraptors may have hunted in packs, using their terrible central claw—almost six inches long—to rip at their prey. "That they're closer to human size and can go into buildings—that makes them all the more frightening," he says.

PRESAGING SCIENCE

Careful research informs Crichton's dinosaur speculations. Paleontologists, however, know Velociraptor as a Mongolian dinosaur closer in size to a poodle than a person. In the film, *Jurassic Park*, it's been sized up and confused with its slightly larger North American cousin, Deinonychus.

But with their raptors, Crichton and Spielberg weren't bucking science, just presaging it. In 1992, Colorado paleontologist James Kirkland announced the discovery of Utahraptor, an earlier and far larger relative of Deinonychus. New discoveries of raptors in Mongolia by American Museum of Natural History scientists also show that some raptor dinosaurs grew at least to *Jurassic Park* proportions.

Horner says the dinosaurs in the film "move just like an animal, not too fast or slow." But as Crichton envisaged them, not even sprinter Carl Lewis is a match for Velociraptors. Indeed, some scientists have theorized dinosaurs sprinting at 50 miles per hour or more. But most scientific estimates of dinosaur speed—made from measuring the stride lengths of dinosaurs from footprints and comparing those to the animal's size—fall far short of Lewis's 25-mile-per-hour dash. According to the trackway evidence, the top speed so far is 25 miles per hour for what seems to have been a medium-sized ornithomimidlike (ostrich mimicking) dinosaur. However, savants of dinosaur locomotion think some dinosaur speed estimates have been widely overestimated.

And must dinosaurs have been hot in order to trot? The raptors of *Jurassic Park* are raging hot-bloods as are the other dinosaurs in the film. But new discoveries of dinosaur metabolism suggest only that some smaller, more active carnivores like Deinonychus may have been hot-blooded in a manner similar to our own metabolism. Other dinosaurs may have switched strategies as they matured, as their growth slowed and their volume grew to proportions that maintained much of their body heat from their bulk alone—without burning calories as expensively as we do. "Dinosaurs probably kept warm," Farlow speculates, adding that dinosaurs' body temperatures might have been as warm as—or warmer than—ours.

Science does not, however, support the speculation of raptors as quick-witted as the sharpest primates. The smartest dinosaur, a more distant relative of the raptors, Troodon, was about as brainy, pound for pound, as an ostrich. That's pretty smart by most animal standards and brighter than our ancestors, the mammals of dinosaur times, but much dimmer than a chimp. "Carnivorous dinosaurs may have been smart enough to pack hunt," Farlow says. "Even some lizards move about in packs." But Southern Methodist University (SMU) paleontologist Louis Jacobs adds, "I can't picture a dinosaur figuring out how to open a door."

Keeping a Real T. Rex

If we ever figure out how to open the doors of genetic engineering wide enough to re-create extinct life, then Jurassic Park, not just its dinosaurs, becomes a possibility and perhaps a reality with which paleontologists and biologists will have to contend. Says Crichton, "I think it's possible we can make a Jurassic Park one day, and I wouldn't be surprised if at some point somebody decided to make one. I hope so. I'd enjoy going very much." So would the scientists who've only been able to study dinosaurs as fossils. "I think it would be pretty cool, though I'd like to see dinosaurs brought back more for study than for entertainment," says Horner.

But just keeping dinosaurs alive, especially on a small island off the coast of Costa Rica, as in *Jurassic Park*, would be a task fraught with problems. Escaping dinosaurs, as in the film, aren't much of a hazard in the eyes of dinosaur scientists or zookeepers of modern-day big animals. "We make T. rex out to be a raging brute, but I doubt they're much more dangerous than a tiger. After all, you can only get bitten to death once," says Farlow. "Seriously, we've learned to handle other large animals from bears to elephants safely. Why not T. rex?"

Not everyone agrees with Farlow. Keeping big animals isn't so safe, says Denver Zoo elephant keeper Liz Hooton. "Bull elephants kill an average of one zookeeper a year worldwide." Still, Hooton thinks a T. rex could be handled. "With positive reinforcement, you can teach any animal." SMU's Jacobs recalls seeing crocodiles trained to come for leftovers tossed into a river in Kenya. But, Hooton adds, "the trick would be not to allow the dinosaurs to associate us too closely with food." Such handouts could cost a keeper a hand or more.

The closest living relatives of T. rex, the raptors, and other carnivorous dinosaurs aren't elephants or other mammals or crocodiles—they're birds. A captive-bird expert, Bill Toone, says, "I think we could keep dinosaurs." Toone is curator of birds, including the endangered condors, at the San Diego Wild Animal Park. Rick Carter, production designer for the film, visited the large, mixed species exhibits at the park while researching *Jurassic Park*. But it's highly unlikely, Toone suggests, that dinosaurs would be allowed to roam widely on a tropical island.

OPTIMAL ENVIRONMENT

A tropical environment would be the best, says Toone, for growing the food the dinosaurs would require because its greenhouselike climate would promote the fastest growth. The real herbivorous dinosaurs were native to temperate rain forests and ate conifers and like plants. But getting enough food for them on a small island would present a problem, as Farlow notes. "There isn't room on a Caribbean island for big herbivores to forage. They'd strip the place clean, and importing the food is expensive." Horner suggests "a bigger island, one that's oriented north-south, since it appears the big dinosaur herbivores migrated that way." He'd try New Zealand. "Of course, we'd have to move the people," he says. And what about the sheep already there? "The dinosaurs would take care of them pretty fast."

It's the nature of the food available for dinosaur herbivores as much as the quantities needed that raise doubts in scientists' minds about dinosaurs browsing in a tropical forest. Just as the Triceratops gets sick from the berries in *Jurassic Park*, real-life paleobotanist Bonnie Jacobs of SMU worries that dinosaurs wouldn't find many familiar foods. "There were no rain forests as we know them in dinosaur times. We do have plants around from the same families dinosaurs knew—tree ferns, monkey-puzzle trees, cycads, ginkgoes, magnolias—all things dinosaurs might eat." But none of these plants lived in the same communities or environments as they do today.

DANGERS TO DINOSAURS

Malnutrition and vitamin deficiencies could easily do in the dinosaurs in a real-life Jurassic Park. Zookeeper Toone suggests keeping the dinosaurs entirely on imported, carefully monitored foods. But even that is no guarantee of health. And Denver zookeeper Hooton says her zoo had an elephant that fell down and never got up. "We didn't realize it had suffered from a vitamin deficiency."

Disease presents another hazard of unknown proportions to keeping dinosaurs. "I'm scared to death of the infection problems," says Toone. "We haven't seen a single infection in 13 years of keeping condors, but we always expect the unexpected." Lots of organisms that present infection problems have evolved since dinosaurs. Big carnivores are especially susceptible to spreading infections since it's hard to get close enough to the animals to check them out.

Carnivorous dinosaurs would likely be kept in small enclosures for training purposes, and in small enclosures, waste becomes a danger to health. "No matter how much you swept, they'd be walking in their own waste," says Hooton, who also points out that in close confinement, you'd have to keep trimming the dinosaurs' feet, since their nails would probably grow too long from lack of proper exercise.

Jack Hanna, director emeritus of the Columbus Zoo, says, "Just cleaning up their crap would be a major problem. With an elephant, it's 40 pounds a day. Who knows how much it would be with a dinosaur. We might have to hire extra keepers just to sweep up."

CLOSE QUARTERS

Each flesh-eating dinosaur would be housed individually and only united with potential mates when both prospective partners showed some interest by nest building or courtship behavior. "It could be the male or the female or both dinosaurs who build the nest and tend the babies. That's how it is with birds," says Toone.

For containing dinosaurs in close quarters, Toone suggests double gates, electric fencing, and steel doors, such as those used to enclose the 40-odd rhinos at the Wild Animal Park. "With patrolling guards and video, you could keep the dinosaurs from getting out and anything else from getting in." Toone says he'd train the dinosaur carnivores by "only giving them food when they went in the 'bedroom'"—a "squeeze gate" constructed of hydraulically operated movable walls.

When rhinos need to be examined by veterinarians, they are temporarily placed in such chutes in order to restrain them without anesthetics. "Anytime you try to tranquilize an animal that big, you risk killing it," Toone says.

So where's the best confined space to keep a live dinosaur? Horner says he'd keep it in a lab. All the safer to do what Farlow and other scientists suggest is the first thing any of them would do with a live dinosaur. "I'd stick a thermometer up it and see how hot it was," says Farlow, thus providing the first experimental proof of a living dinosaur's metabolism.

Perhaps then we'd know how accurate *Jurassic Park*'s dinosaurs really are. For now, neither science nor *Jurassic Park* can tell us what dinosaur were like or how we might keep them in zoos. However, as Crichton points out, "keeping dinosaurs is just a metaphor in *Jurassic Park*. Science is trying to do something that's beneficial, but it screws up. If we bring dinosaurs or anything else to life, we have a responsibility because we made them this time. They're our animals."

FOR FURTHER RESEARCH

Novels by Michael Crichton

The Andromeda Strain. New York: Knopf, 1969.

The Terminal Man. New York: Knopf, 1972.

Westworld. New York: Bantam, 1974.

The Great Train Robbery. New York: Knopf, 1975.

Eaters of the Dead. New York: Knopf, 1976.

Congo. New York: Knopf, 1980.

Sphere. New York: Knopf, 1987.

Jurassic Park. New York: Knopf, 1990.

Rising Sun. New York: Knopf, 1992.

Disclosure. New York: Knopf, 1994.

The Lost World. New York: Knopf, 1995.

Airframe. New York: Knopf, 1996.

Timeline. New York: Knopf, 1999.

Prey. New York: Knopf, 2002.

Nonfiction by Michael Crichton

Five Patients: The Hospital Explained. New York: Knopf, 1970.

Jasper Johns. New York: Abrams, 1977.

Electronic Life: How to Think About Computers. New York: Knopf, 1983.

Travels. New York: Knopf, 1988.

Screenplays by Michael Crichton

Pursuit. ABC TV, 1972.

Extreme Close-Up [aka *Sex Through a Window*]. National General, 1973.

Westworld. Metro-Goldwyn-Mayer, 1973.

Coma. United Artists, 1977.

The Great Train Robbery. United Artists, 1979.

Looker. Warner Bros., 1981.

Runaway. Tri-Star Pictures, 1984.

Twister, with Anne-Marie Martin. Warner Bros., 1996.

Pseudonym Novels by Michael Crichton

John Lange, *Odds On.* New York: New American Library, 1966.

———, *Scratch One.* New York: New American Library, 1967.

———, *Easy Go.* New York: New American Library, 1968. Published as *The Last Tomb.* New York: Bantam, 1974.

———, *Zero Cool.* New York: New American Library, 1969.

———, *The Venom Business.* New York: New American Library, 1969.

———, *Drug of Choice.* New York: New American Library, 1970.

———, *Grave Descend.* New York: New American Library, 1970.

———, *Binary.* New York: Knopf, 1971.

Jeffrey Hudson, *A Case of Need.* New York: New American Library, 1968.

Michael Douglas, with Douglas Crichton, *Dealing: Or, the Berkeley-to-Boston Forty-Brick Lost-Bag Blues.* New York: Knopf, 1971.

Films Directed by Michael Crichton

Pursuit [aka *Binary*]. ABC TV, 1972.

Westworld. Metro-Goldwyn-Mayer, 1973.

Coma. United Artists, 1977.

The Great Train Robbery. United Artists, 1979.

Looker. Warner Bros., 1981.

Runaway. Tri-Star Pictures, 1984.

Physical Evidence. Columbia Pictures, 1989.

The 13th Warrior (reshoots; uncredited). Touchstone Pictures, Walt Disney Pictures, 1999.

Games by Michael Crichton

Amazon. Telarium, 1984.

Academic Writing on Michael Crichton

Warren Buckland, "Between Science Fact and Science Fiction: Spielberg's Digital Dinosaurs, Possible Worlds, and the New Aesthetic Realism," *Screen 40*, Summer 1999.

Floyd D. Cheung, "Imagining Danger, Imagining Nation: Postcolonial Discourse in *Rising Sun* and *Stargate*," *Jouvert: A Journal of Postcolonial Studies*, vol. 2, issue 2, 1998.

Nigel Clark, "Panic Ecology: Nature in the Age of Superconductivity," *Theory Culture & Society*, February 1997.

Gilberto Diaz-Santos, "Technothrillers and English for Science and Technology," *English for Specific Purposes*, vol. 14, issue 3, 2000.

Harriett Hawkins, "Paradigms Lost: Chaos, Milton, and *Jurassic Park*," *Textual Practice*, Summer 1994.

Burton Kendle, "Lean Dickens and Admirable Crichton: Film Adaptations of Literature," *Michigan Academician*, January 1996.

Edward A. Kopper Jr., "Conrad in Michael Crichton's *Sphere*," *Notes on Contemporary Literature*, September 1989.

Allen Michie, "New Historicism and *Jurassic Park*," *Notes on Teaching English*, vol. 25, issue 1, 1997.

Valerie S. Terry and Edward Schiappa, "Disclosing Antifeminism in Michael Crichton's Postfeminist *Disclosure*," *Journal of Communication Inquiry*, January 1999.

Carol Watts, "Thinking *Disclosure:* Or, the Structure of Post-Feminist Cynicism," *Women: A Cultural Review*, Winter 1995.

Selected Popular Press Publications About Michael Crichton

Robert W. Lucky, "Fact or Fiction?" *IEEE Spectrum*, July 2001.

New York Times, "Back in the Land of Dinosaur Cloning," October 10, 1995.

———, "Is Japan Really Out to Get Us?" February 9, 1992.

———, "A Time Traveler Returns, Still Restless," November 24, 1999.

Jesse Posner, "*Lost World*'s Master: Michael Crichton," *Fast Times*, May 1997.

Scott Rosenberg, "Mediasaurus Wrecks," *Salon*, December 9, 1996.

Saturday Review, "A Tall Storyteller," November/December 1984.

Sight & Sound, "The Admirable Crichton," February 2001.

Spectator, "Sometime After Dinosaurs, God Created Woman," January 22, 1994.

Time, "How Good Is His Science?" September 25, 1995.

Elizabeth A. Trembley, *Michael Crichton: A Critical Companion*. Westport, CT: Greenwood Press, 1994.

Websites

Complete Review, www.complete-review.com. This site provides comprehensive listings and summaries of book reviews of many authors, including Michael Crichton.

Crichton.org, www.crichton.org. This site offers numerous items for fans of Michael Crichton, including published articles and features (many written by Crichton), news, biographical information, and discussion boards.

MichaelCrichton.net, www.crichton-official.com. Michael Crichton's official website offers visitors information about each of his works, including commentary by Crichton. Also includes pictures, message boards, press releases, special features, and news.

Stephan's Retrocomputing Site, www.retrosite.de. In 1984 Michael Crichton wrote a video game called *Amazon*, a graphical text adventure game. Information on the game, including screenshots and downloadable files, are found here.

Where the Meteor Scarred Arizona's Desert, http://members. aol.com/amwso/crichton/NYTarticle.html. This site posts the travel piece Michael Crichton wrote for the *New York Times* when he was fourteen.

INDEX

Airframe, 27, 41, 47, 53
Andromeda Strain, The, 11, 20, 33, 36–37, 44, 48
Andromeda Strain, The (film), 22–23, 93
Arnold, Gary, 91
awards, 36

Binary (Lange), 20, 21, 44–45
book collecting, 49–51
book signings, 54
Brown, Corie, 39

career
  as director, 23, 45, 49, 91–96
  early, 19–21, 33–37, 42–45
  slump, 24–26, 45–46, 52–53
  successes, 14–15, 26–28, 46–47
Carey Treatment, The (film), 20, 44
Carter, Rick, 114
Case of Need, A (Hudson), 20, 21, 36, 43–44
Centesis, 52
characters
  are caricatures, 76–77
  lackluster, 77
  name of, 47–48
  poor development of, 58
childhood, 15–17, 35, 42–43
Childs, Suzanne, 29
cinematic storytelling, 12–13
Coma (film), 17, 23, 45, 95
Congo, 25
Connelly, Julie, 75
Constant C Productions, 52

craft novels, 79–83
Crichton, Douglas (brother), 38, 45
Crichton, John Henderson (father), 15, 16, 35
Crichton, Michael, 97
  artistic influences on, 48–49, 65–67, 92
  awards received by, 36
  childhood of, 15–17, 35, 42–43
  college experience of, 17–18
  directing career of, 23, 45, 49, 91–96
  early career of, 19–21, 33–37, 42–45
  early passions of, 17
  early writing by, 15, 43
  family life of, 29–30, 46–47
  future prospects for, 31
  height of, 16–17
  influence of father on, 15, 35
  interviews with, 47–54, 91–96
  marriages of, 29–30, 46–47
  in medical school, 18–19, 21–22, 34
  portrayal of science/scientists by, 97–106
  relationship with father and, 16, 29
  spiritual matters and, 28–29
  successes of, 14–15, 26–28, 46–47
  travels of, 25, 35–36
  unsuccessful period of, 24–26, 45–46, 52–53
  versatility of, 39–41

writing skills of, 11–13
Crichton, Taylor Ann (daughter), 30
Crichton, Zula (Miller) (mother), 15, 95

Dealing: Or the Berkeley-to-Boston Forty-Brick Lost-Bag Blues, 45
dinosaurs
  authenticity of, in *Jurassic Park*, 108–17
  scientific knowledge about, 110–17
Disclosure, 27, 75–78
Douglas, Michael (pseudonym), 19, 45
Drucker, Peter, 74
Drug of Choice (Lange), 44
Dugdale, John, 83

Eaters of the Dead, 24–25
electronic books, 51
Electronic Life, 25, 51
epigraphs, 52
ER (TV series), 11, 27, 47
Extreme Close-Up (film), 23, 45

Fail-Safe, 37
fame, changes due to, 34–35
Farlow, James, 110, 111, 113–15, 117
Five Patients, 24, 45
Frankenstein (Shelley), 65–66

Grave Descend (Lange), 44
Great Train Robbery, The, 24, 45
Great Train Robbery, The (film), 23, 95

Hanna, Jack, 116
Hitchcock, Alfred, 17, 92
Hooton, Liz, 114, 115
Horner, John R., 108, 110, 114
Hudson, Jeffrey (pseudonym), 19, 36, 43

Island of Dr. Moreau, The (Wells), 66

Jacobs, Bonnie, 115
Japanese, view of, presented in *Rising Sun*, 68–74
Jasper Johns, 24, 50
Johns, Jasper, 48
Jones, Malcolm, 39
Jurassic Park, 26, 53, 62–67
Jurassic Park (film)
  authenticity of, 108–10
  behind-the-scenes look at, 107–17
  portrayal of scientists in, 100–101
  science in, 101–104
  success of, 11, 12–13, 26–27

Kahn, James M., 59
Kippen, David, 42
Klinghoffer, David, 79

Lange, John (pseudonym), 19, 36, 43, 52
Last Tomb, The, 43
Lessem, Don, 107
Looker (film), 23, 52
Lost World, The (film), 27, 47

marriages, 29–30, 46–47
Martin, Anne-Marie (wife), 27, 29–30, 47
medical school, 18–19, 21–22, 34
multiple sclerosis, 22

novels
  craft, 79–83
  selling strategies for, 40
  subject matters of, 12
  unsuccessful, 24–26, 45–46
  written under pseudonyms, 19–21, 36, 43–44, 49–50
  see also specific titles

Odds On, 43
out-of-body experiences, 29
Ovitz, Michael, 40

Physical Evidence (film), 23, 46
Prey, 28, 86–89
pseudonyms, 19, 36, 37, 43–44, 52
Pursuit (TV film), 23, 45

Radam, Joan, 29
Rising Sun, 27, 68–74
Roth, Joe, 41
Runaway (film), 23, 52–53

Sawhill, Ray, 39
science/scientists
  flaws of, 99–100
  misunderstand the media, 98–99, 101–102
  portrayal of, in movies, 97–106
Scratch One (Lange), 36, 43
Shelley, Mary, 65–66
Shenker, Israel, 33
Sphere, 25, 59–61
Spielberg, Steven, 14, 23, 47, 83, 109
spiritual matters, 28–29
St. Johns, Kathy, 29
Stone, Oliver, 68, 70
Sturgeon, Theodore, 56
subject matters, 12
suspense, development of, 62–67

television shows, 35
  ER, 11, 27, 47
  Pursuit, 23, 45
  Terminal Man, The, 24, 45, 48, 56–58
Tharp, Mike, 72
Timeline, 39
  film deal for, 40–41
  is formulaic, 83–85
  is good craft novel, 79–83
  plot of, 27–28
  reviews of, 79–85
  writing skill in, 12
To Catch a Thief (film), 92
Toone, Bill, 114, 115, 116–17
Travels, 16, 25–26, 29, 46
Trembley, Elizabeth A., 62
20,000 Leagues Under the Sea (Verne), 61
Twister (film), 27, 47
Tyrannosaurus rex, 110–11, 114

Venom Business, The (Lange), 44
Verne, Jules, 61
Vizzini, Ned, 86

Wells, H.G., 66
Westworld (film), 23, 45
Will, George F., 68
Wise, Robert, 23
writer's block, 24–25

Zero Cool (Lange), 44